THE NEW IRISH TABLE

THE NEW IRISH TABLE

70 CONTEMPORARY RECIPES

BY MARGARET M. JOHNSON

PHOTOGRAPHS BY MARGARET M. JOHNSON
FOOD PHOTOGRAPHS BY CHRISTOPHER HIRSHEIMER

CHRONICLE BOOKS
SAN FRANCISCO

Library of Congress Cataloging-in-Publication Data:
Johnson, Margaret M., 1944–
    The new Irish table : 70 contemporary recipes / by Margaret M. Johnson; photographs
    by Margaret M. Johnson ; food photographs by Christopher Hirsheimer.
        p. cm.
        Includes index.
        ISBN 0-8118-3387-9 (paperback)
        1. Cookery, Irish. I. Title.
    TX717.5 .J6423 2003

Manufactured in China.

Credits:
The recipes for Crab and Champ Bake with Tomato-Watercress Dressing (page 52), and
Baked Rock Oysters with Bacon, Cabbage, and Guinness Sabayon (page 60), were used
with permission of Bord Bia (Irish Food Board).
The recipe for Goat Cheese and Roasted Tomato Charlotte (page 55) was used with
permission of Atrium Books, Cork, Ireland.
The recipe for Medallions of Beef with Port Sauce and Cashel Blue Cheese (page 89) was
used with permission of the Cork Simon Community, publishers of *The Cork Cook Book.*
The recipe for Baileys Baked Alaskas on Madeira Cake (page 137) was used with permis-
sion of Baileys Irish Cream and *Baileys Pure Indulgence*, published by Baileys.
The recipe for Rustic Apple Tart with Hazelnut Crumble (page 151) was used with permis-
sion of Fuschia Brands Ltd. and *The West Cork Leader.*
The recipe for Chocolate Mousse Cake (page 138) was used with permission of Smurfit
Communications' *Food & Wine* magazine, Dublin, Ireland.

Food styling by Melissa Hamilton. Assistant food stylist Julia Lee.
Designed by Eliza Mayo, and pdbd.
Typesetting by pdbd.

Page 2: Dunmanus Bay, County Cork; Spicy Pear Tart, page 146.
Page 6: The Wild Geese Restaurant, Adare, County Limerick.
Page 7: Kinsale, County Cork.
Page 9: Durrus, County Cork.

Distributed in Canada by:
Raincoast Books
9050 Shaughnessy Street
Vancouver, BC V6P 6E5

10 9 8 7 6 5 4 3 2 1

Chronicle Books LLC
85 Second Street
San Francisco, California 94105

www.chroniclebooks.com

For dear friends Mairéad McCarthy O'Sullivan, Kerry and Cork; and Chef Noel McMeel, Antrim

ACKNOWLEDGMENTS

I'D LIKE TO express my thanks to the chefs, hoteliers, restaurateurs, and Irish home cooks who contributed recipes and advice for this book; to Bord Bia (Irish Food Board) in Chicago and Dublin, for their inspiration; to Bord Fáilte (Irish Tourist Board) in New York and Dublin, for their support; to Bord Bainne (Irish Dairy Board) in Chicago and Dublin; to CAIS, the Irish Farmhouse Cheesemakers Association; Fionnuala Jay-O'Boyle, A Taste of Ulster; Jillian Bolger, editor, Ireland's *Food & Wine* magazine; Philip McGauran, Belvedere Communications; my agent, Madeleine Morel, who guided me through the writing process; Bill LeBlond, Editorial Director, Cookbooks, Chronicle Books, for his faith in me again; Amy Treadwell, Chronicle Books, for her assistance; and to my husband, Carl, for his indulgence in all things Irish!

TABLE OF CONTENTS

INTRODUCTION

WHEN I FIRST visited Ireland in 1984, I began a love affair with the place where my grandparents and great-grandparents were born. I loved the people, the landscape, the history, the folklore, and the music, but I must admit the affection didn't extend to my palate.

My children, aged nine and seven at the time, were enchanted by the wooly sheep and languid cows that slowed traffic on country lanes and brushed by our car close enough to touch, and they were thrilled at the carnival atmosphere of Kerry's ancient Puck Fair in Killorglin: the bumper cars, the carousel rides, and the big goat perched high above the square in whose honor the fair is held. My husband developed an insatiable appetite for the golf courses of the west of Ireland—Ballybunion, Lahinch, Waterville—and for pints of Guinness at pubs named Donahoe's, McCarthy's, and Hennessy's. We all treasured Ireland for reasons of our own, but none of us thought much about the food, except breakfast, perhaps, when we would sit down

with total strangers and be fussed over about how we wanted our eggs cooked, and did we want a bit of porridge to start, or did we need more toast and jam?

To be honest, when you travel to a foreign country with young children, you look more for golden arches than for Michelin stars, so our 1984 visit to Ireland was not exactly a gourmet tour. We ate simple foods like Irish stew, fish 'n' chips, and sandwiches made with thick slabs of ham and slices of Cheddar cheese, and we still came home raving about all things Irish. Serious food was irrelevant.

For years after that first trip, a day never passed when I didn't think of Ireland. Thanks to my Irish-born grandmother, I eventually had my name registered in the Foreign Births Record and was issued an Irish passport. I've traveled there more than two dozen times in the last ten years, and with each new visit I've grown to love Ireland more: the people, the landscape, the history, the folklore, the music, and, *finally*, the food.

Athlone, County Westmeath.

I'd like to think that my newfound appreciation of Irish food was some kind of personal epiphany, but, frankly, a "gastronomic revolution" was taking place all the while. Food fairs and festivals were beginning to blossom, gourmet food markets were flourishing, artisan cheese makers were growing in number, and there was a constant buzz about new restaurants opening and who was in charge of the kitchen. I started to plan entire visits around destinations where I'd heard about the food, and learned from Irish friends where to find the best. I visited Ballymaloe, the legendary Cork country

home that virtually changed the perception that people had of Irish food, and chatted with hostess Myrtle Allen, one of the first of the country's cooks to promote the use of native and local ingredients.

In Dublin, people were talking about Patrick Guilbaud and his new French restaurant. Restaurants called L'Ecrivain, Les Frères Jacques, and La Mère Zou would eventually follow. Was Dublin experiencing a French Revolution, too? Not quite, because traditional Irish food was being drawn into the food equation as well, and places like Gallagher's opened in Dublin's Temple Bar and built an entire menu around boxty, a traditional County Leitrim potato pancake. Boxty remains the specialty of the house and is served with country fare like diced bacon and cabbage, beef and stout, lamb and potatoes. Irish stew was suddenly fashionable!

In Cork, Val Manning began hosting the West Cork Food Fair to showcase local products. There we sampled fine farmhouse cheeses lovingly sliced by their makers—Bill Hogan, Giana Ferguson, Helene Willems among them—and visited Veronica and Norman Steele's hilltop farm in Eyeries, where Milleens, Ireland's first officially recognized farmhouse cheese, originated. We drank coffee on their stone patio before Veronica showed us how she makes her Camembert-style cheese in a small building behind her home. She told us about her one-horned cow named Brisket, who produced so much milk Veronica was almost forced into the cheese business just to use up the surplus! Others followed, and now there are more than thirty members of CAIS, the Irish Farmhouse Cheesemakers Association, producing Irish versions of international favorites like Brie, Camembert, Gouda, and Cheddar.

Food initiatives like A Taste of Wicklow and Taste of Ulster were launched to highlight regional cuisines, and in 1994 the Irish government established Bord

Bia/The Irish Food Board to promote Irish foods and beverages worldwide. The premiere issue of the country's stylish, glossy *Food & Wine* magazine arrived in June 1997 affirming the new Irish lifestyle, which increasingly revolves around fine cuisine from across the country and around the world, and in 2001 Bord Bia introduced Feile Bia/A Festival of Food, which encourages restaurants in Ireland to develop dishes and menus to profile local food, drink, and artisan products.

Only a generation ago, the world perceived the Irish diet to be little more than a pint of Guinness and a bowl of stew—or as Kevin Kelly, the founding publisher of *Food & Wine* put it: "The Irish themselves had for too long been fobbed off with less than appetizing fare from often dark and dingy pubs or hotels."

Today, people are buzzing about a "new" Irish cuisine. The days of the bad jokes about Irish food are finally over, and the inert image of Irish cooking—its legacy of famine, emigration, wars, and the Troubles—is slowly being eclipsed by a more modern, inspired, and cosmopolitan approach. So, no more proletarian pub grub? No more rustic simplicity and hearty cooking? No more bacon and cabbage, soda bread and scones, bangers and mash? Not a chance!

Well, then, what is this "new Irish cuisine," I'm constantly asked. What are the new tastes from the Irish table, and how did the image of Irish cooking change?

I think the best answer is this: Irish cuisine is a style of cooking that uses local ingredients and is based on traditional dishes. In 1968, Irish food writer Theodora FitzGibbons declared: "The best food of a country is the traditional food which has been tried and tested over the centuries. It's food that suits the climate and uses the best products of that country. . . . It's part of its history and civilization, and, ideally, the past and the present should be combined so that traditional food

is not lost under a pile of tins or packages."

New Irish chefs came to recognize that there was nothing wrong with the basic ingredients of their cooking—some of the best beef, lamb, and pork in the world; fresh fish; incomparable dairy products; wild fruits and berries; vegetables, especially the potato, the country's great staple—but that they had to learn to broaden their tastes and apply more sophisticated, international cooking techniques to the marvelous bounty of their homeland. Eventually, more and more chefs have come to embrace and develop this style of cooking, experiment with new dishes based on traditional foods, and serve them with touches from Asian, Mediterranean, and Latin American cuisines.

In a country that has become arguably the most dynamic place in Europe—it boasts an economy that outpaces all others, is one of the most popular tourist destinations for visitors from the Continent, and saw the number of visitors from North America grow to one million in 2000—it comes as no surprise that food in Ireland has kept pace with these dynamics and has taken on a distinctive new identity.

The New Irish Table will show you how the food of Ireland, often used in Irish literature to provide focus, punctuation, rhythm, and in some instances, entire plots, has moved boldly into the new millennium, no longer, as James Joyce once wrote, "an outcast from life's feast."

With more than seventy inspired and innovative recipes in five chapters—tasty tidbits like crostini with black pudding; appetizing starters like crabmeat soufflés; hearty main courses of lamb, pork, and beef; inventive potato and vegetables dishes; and decadent desserts ranging from steamed puddings to crème brûlée—*The New Irish Table* offers exciting tastes from modern Ireland and deliciously defines today's Irish cuisine.

Bain taitneamh as do bhéile! Bon appétit!

SMALL BITES

Opposite, top: Schull, County Cork. Opposite, bottom: Ballyvourney, County Cork

Crackers and cheese are the quintessential party food, and homemade Cheddar crackers are a snap to make in a food processor. Serve them with a variety of pâtés and spreads, and present a cheese board with chutneys.

CHEDDAR CRACKERS

1¾ cups all-purpose flour

½ teaspoon baking powder

1¼ teaspoons dry mustard

½ teaspoon salt

½ cup (1 stick) cold unsalted butter, cut into small pieces

1 cup (4 ounces) shredded Cheddar cheese, preferably Kerrygold Vintage Cheddar

2 to 3 tablespoons ice water

Sesame seeds (optional)

In a food processor, combine the flour, baking powder, mustard, and salt. Pulse 2 to 3 times to blend. Add the butter. Pulse 5 to 10 times, or until the mixture resembles coarse crumbs. Add the cheese and 2 tablespoons of the water. Process for 1 to 2 minutes, or until the dough comes together. Add 1 tablespoon more water, if needed, to make the dough manageable. Turn the dough out onto a lightly floured work surface, shape it into a ball, then cut it in half and form into 2 disks. Wrap them in plastic wrap and refrigerate for 30 minutes.

Preheat the oven to 350°F. Grease 2 baking sheets.

On a lightly floured work surface, roll half the dough out to a ¼-inch thickness. Using a 2½-inch cookie cutter, cut out rounds. Re-roll and cut out more rounds, until all the dough has been used. Repeat the process with the second disk.

Place the rounds 2 inches apart on the prepared pans. Sprinkle with sesame seeds, if you wish. Bake for 10 to 12 minutes, or until the edges are lightly browned. Transfer the crackers to wire racks and let cool completely. Store in an airtight container for up to 3 days.

MAKES ABOUT 26 CRACKERS

Like oysters, which connoisseurs prefer in their most natural state, oak-smoked Irish salmon is often eaten simply with a squeeze of lemon and a slice of brown bread. But its flavor pairs so well with other ingredients, it's no surprise to also find it in a pâté, atop roasted potatoes, or combined with blue cheese and fresh spinach in these tartlets from David Foley, chef-owner of the Wild Geese Restaurant in picturesque Adare, County Limerick. Chef Foley fills handmade pastry cases with the mixture, but these use frozen filo dough shells.

CASHEL BLUE, SPINACH, AND SMOKED SALMON TARTLETS

2 packages frozen mini filo dough shells

½ cup packed fresh spinach leaves

¾ cup half-and-half

2 eggs

Freshly ground pepper to taste

2 ounces Cashel Blue cheese, or other blue cheese, cut into small pieces (about ½ cup)

1 ounce smoked salmon, preferably Irish, finely chopped

Preheat the oven to 350°F. Remove the frozen filo shells from the package, place on a baking sheet, and let sit at room temperature for 10 minutes.

Cook the spinach in salted boiling water for 2 to 3 minutes, or until wilted. Drain, rinse in cold water, and squeeze dry. Chop coarsely.

In a large bowl, whisk the half-and-half, eggs, and pepper together. Stir in the spinach, blue cheese, and smoked salmon. Spoon 1 teaspoon of the mixture into each shell. Bake for 12 to 15 minutes, or until set.

MAKES 30 TARTLETS

An Irish Cheese Board

In the 1970s, a natural revival of farmhouse cheese making began in Ireland on land that had been farmed by the same families for generations, and on small holdings bought by people who wanted to escape to the peace of the Irish countryside. The first cheeses were made to satisfy the desire for more interesting food than was then available, and later ones were developed by European expatriates who had moved to Ireland and missed their native cheeses.

With nearly fifty farmhouse cheeses being crafted in Ireland today—along with others made by commercial dairies—a cheese board is the best way to appreciate Irish cheese and is perfect party fare.

Offer at least one or two farmhouse cheeses from each of the major categories: a soft or semisoft surface-ripened or washed-rind cheese like Abbey Brie, Ardrahan, Cooleeney, Durrus, Dunbarra, Gubbeen, Lavistown, Milleens, St. Killian, and Yeats Country; a semifirm, waxed-rind cheese like Bay-Lough, Carrigaline, Coolea, Kerry Farmhouse, Killorglin, Knockanore, Mont Bellair, and Riverville Farmhouse; a blue-veined cheese like Abbey Blue Brie, Bellingham, Cashel Blue, Crozier Blue, and Oisin Farmhouse Blue; a goat or

sheep cheese like Corbetstown, Corleggy, Cratloe Hills, Knockalara, Mine-Gabhar, Oisin Farmhouse, Poulcoin, or St. Tola; and a well-aged hard cheese like Desmond or Gabriel. Commercially made Blarney, Dubliner, Kerrygold Swiss, and Tipperary Cheddar are also nice additions.

Several cheese makers make smoked cheeses (Abbey smoked Brie, Ardrahan, Bay-Lough, Gubbeen, Knockanore, and Riverville Farmhouse), while others produce herb-flavored varieties like Bay-Lough, with garlic and herbs; Cahill's herb blend; Coolea, with cumin; Kerry Farmhouse, with garlic, chives, nettles, and hazelnuts; and Knockanore, flavored with garlic and herbs, black pepper, and chives.

For a one-of-a-kind cheese experience, add one of the adventurous waxed-round Cheddars from Cahill's Farm Cheese: Ballintubber, with chives; Ballyporeen, with mixed Irish herbs; Vintage Cheddar, with hazelnuts; and three others marbled with red wine, stout, and Irish whiskey respectively.

Temple Bar Market, Dublin.

Sheridans Cheesemongers, Dublin.

Offer at least 2 ounces of cheese per person on a cheese board. Cut cheeses for each portion while cold, but bring to room temperature before serving. Arrange generous wedges of cheese on a large plate, wooden board, or piece of marble and provide several knives: a wide blade for semi-firm cheeses like Coolea, a curved spreader for soft-ripened cheeses like Milleens, a thin blade for semisoft cheeses like Gubbeen, a heart-shaped blade for hard cheeses like Gabriel, a cheese wire for cutting blues so they don't crumble, and a forked cheese knife for picking up precut pieces. If you have a large wedge of cheese cut from a whole wheel, a cheese plane is ideal for shaving off thin slices.

In Ireland, cheese is often served with chutney, or paired with fresh fruits like green apples, pears, and grapes, or with dried fruits like figs or apricots. Toasted almonds, pistachios, and walnuts are easy accompaniments, too, along with pumpernickel and brown soda bread, bread sticks, crackers, and biscuits. See Resources (page 161) for details on where to buy Irish cheeses.

As party fare, pâtés and spreads are easy to make and elegant to serve accompanied with crackers and biscuits, slices of soda bread, crostini, or toast. Packed in crocks, ramekins, or molds of varying sizes, most can be made up to a day or more in advance, and the recipes can easily be doubled or tripled depending on the number of servings.

SMOKED SALMON PÂTÉ

1 tablespoon unsalted butter

12 ounces flounder or sole fillets

1 tablespoon fresh lime juice

1 tablespoon minced fresh flat-leaf parsley

1 tablespoon minced fresh chives

1 teaspoon minced fresh dill

One 3-ounce package cream cheese at room temperature

8 ounces sliced smoked salmon, preferably Irish, chopped

4 dill sprigs for garnish

In a small skillet, melt the butter over low heat. Add the fillets and cook for 3 to 5 minutes, turning once, or until opaque throughout. Transfer to a cutting board and cut into pieces.

In a food processor, combine the fish, pan juices, lime juice, parsley, chives, and dill and process for 20 to 30 seconds, or until smooth. Add the cream cheese and salmon, and process again until well combined. Divide the mixture among four lightly oiled 6-ounce ramekins, cover with plastic wrap, and refrigerate for at least 4 hours or overnight. To serve, unmold onto serving plates and garnish with dill sprigs.

SERVES 6 TO 8

St. Colman's Cathedral, Cobh, County Cork.

The Smokehouse

Smoked Irish salmon acquires its inimitable dark orange color and subtle flavor from the traditional method of smoking over an open wood fire or in a kiln. It can be smoked horizontally on trays, or suspended over an oak or beechwood fire.

There are countless smokehouses in Ireland where salmon is smoked using both methods, but the flavor and texture is determined by the quality of the fish, whether wild, organic, or conventionally farmed. Wild salmon is caught in its natural habitat and is the most expensive due to its increasing scarcity. Because it gets so much exercise returning from its natural feeding grounds in the North Atlantic to native rivers to spawn, it tends to have extra muscle and denser flesh. Wild salmon may be legally caught and sold in Ireland for only thirty-two days a year, during June and July.

Conventionally farmed salmon are confined to cages, and chemicals are sometimes added to their feed. Organic salmon are raised in a farm environment that resembles the natural habitat of the fish, with a stock density much lower than that of other farms. For the most part, the cages are located in waters off the western coast of Ireland, where there's a high tidal exchange and strong currents that compel the salmon to swim. Such strong exercise results in fish with a firm flesh and a lower fat content. The use of dyes, pesticides, artificial additives, and antibiotics is forbidden.

The smoking is the final phase in the process. First, the fish is salted, which cures and preserves it, killing off any bacteria and drawing out moisture; drying, where the salt is washed off and the salmon is air-dried; and, finally, the smoking, which can take up to thirty-five hours. Vacuum packaging gives Irish smoked salmon a shelf life of about twenty-eight days when refrigerated.

See Resources (page 161) for details on where to buy oak-smoked Irish salmon.

Like salmon, smoked trout is a popular fish in Ireland, and it combines well with creamy ingredients like mayonnaise, yogurt, or hard-cooked eggs for a spread. Try this on brown bread, crackers, or toast rounds.

SMOKED TROUT AND DILL SPREAD

2 smoked trout, skinned, boned, and crumbled

½ cup finely chopped red onion

½ cup mayonnaise

2 tablespoons minced fresh dill, or 1 tablespoon dried dill

4 teaspoons prepared horseradish

1 tablespoon fresh lemon juice

2 teaspoons Worcestershire sauce

Ground white pepper to taste

4 hard-cooked eggs, 2 coarsely chopped and 2 cut into wedges

Line two 2½-cup molds with plastic wrap. In a food processor, combine the trout, onion, mayonnaise, dill, horseradish, lemon juice, Worcestershire sauce, and pepper. Process for 20 to 30 seconds, or until well blended. Stir in the chopped eggs. Spoon the mixture into the prepared molds, cover with plastic wrap, and refrigerate for at least 2 hours or up to 24 hours.

To serve, invert the molds onto a serving plate and garnish with the egg wedges.

SERVES 6 TO 8

Potatoes have always been Irish comfort food, and today they're sophisticated finger food, too, versatile enough to be combined with luxurious ingredients like blue cheese, caviar, and smoked salmon.

ROASTED NEW POTATOES

24 evenly sized new potatoes (Yukon Gold or Red Bliss)

1½ tablespoons olive oil

2 tablespoons sea salt

¾ cup sour cream

1 tablespoon minced fresh chives

1½ teaspoons minced fresh dill

Freshly ground pepper to taste

4 ounces black caviar, or smoked salmon, minced

Preheat the oven to 425°F. Put the potatoes in a shallow baking dish. Add the olive oil and sea salt and toss until well coated. Bake for 20 to 25 minutes, or until potatoes are tender. Cut a small slice off the bottom of each potato so that it will stand upright. With a teaspoon-sized measuring spoon or a melon baller, scoop out a hollow in the center of each potato. (The potatoes can be prepared up to this point 2 hours ahead. Let stand at room temperature, then reheat in a preheated 425°F oven for 15 minutes before filling.)

In a small bowl, combine the sour cream, chives, dill, and pepper. Stir to blend. Put a teaspoonful into each hollowed potato, top with caviar or salmon, and serve immediately.

MAKES 24

Black and White Puddings from Clonakilty

The first reference to black and white puddings, or sausages, was in 44 B.C. in *Apicius*, the first known cookbook. They were first introduced to France, and later to England and Ireland. Black pudding is named for its color, derived from pig's blood, which is mixed with oatmeal, then seasoned, stuffed into a casing, formed into a large coil, and boiled. Black pudding is usually cut into thick pieces, then fried or grilled as part of an Irish breakfast. White pudding is made from minced pork, pinhead (steel-cut) oatmeal, and spices. Both are grainy, nutty, and flavorful.

Philip Harrington developed his pudding recipes in his butcher shop at 16 Sovereign Street (now Pearse Street) in Clonakilty, County Cork, in the 1890s. Years later, Edward Twomey took over the shop and the recipe from Harrington, and the Clonakilty brand remains Ireland's best known.

Clonakilty, County Cork.

Modern cooks update the puddings by serving them grilled, with foods of contrasting flavors like apple, bacon, potatoes, and wild mushrooms. See Resources (page 161) for details on where to buy black and white puddings.

Black and white puddings have been the mainstay of Irish breakfasts for generations, served alongside bacon, eggs, and sausages. Today, black pudding, the most famous of which is the grainy, loose-textured version from Clonakilty, County Cork, is grilled and served on crostini with a spoonful of applesauce. The Clonakilty brand is not exported to the United States, but Galtee makes a similar version.

CROSTINI WITH BLACK PUDDING AND APPLESAUCE

6 tablespoons olive oil

12 slices black pudding

Twelve ½-inch-thick baguette slices

4 tablespoons chunky applesauce

In a large skillet over medium heat, heat 2 tablespoons of the olive oil. Fry the pudding slices 3 to 5 minutes on each side, or until browned. Using a slotted metal spatula, transfer to paper towels to drain.

Preheat the broiler. Brush the remaining 4 tablespoons olive oil on the bread slices and brown under the broiler on each side for 1 to 2 minutes, or until lightly toasted. Top each toast with a slice of pudding and put a teaspoonful of applesauce on top. Serve immediately.

MAKES 12 SERVINGS

The boatlike shape of Belgian endive leaves makes them great for stuffing, and their slightly bitter flavor pairs well with a smooth blend of cream cheese and Abbey Blue Brie. Pipe the cheese mix into the leaves and serve with a sprinkling of walnuts.

ENDIVE AND BLUE CHEESE CANAPÉS

Two 3-ounce packages cream cheese
    at room temperature

¼ cup sour cream

1 tablespoon minced fresh flat-leaf
    parsley

Pinch of salt

4 ounces Abbey Blue Brie cheese or
    other blue Brie, cut into small pieces
    (about 1 cup)

40 Belgian endive leaves (about
    5 heads), rinsed and dried

2 tablespoons chopped walnuts

In a food processor, combine the cream cheese, sour cream, parsley, salt, and blue Brie. Process for 30 to 40 seconds, or until smooth. Spoon the mixture into a large pastry bag and squeeze a strip onto each endive leaf. Sprinkle with chopped walnuts. Refrigerate for 30 minutes.

MAKES 40 CANAPÉS

Irish Cheese and Wine

Pairing Irish cheeses with wine is a sophisticated idea for entertaining a small group of friends, and a delicious way to do it is by taking a cheese "flight," similar to what you might do in a wine bar where you sample three or more wines from the same grape variety or from the same vintage.

A cheese flight involves sampling small portions of several cheeses that have something in common, such as cheese from the same family or age group, like Cheddars, blues, soft cheese, or extra-aged cheese.

A soft-ripened cheese flight (bloomy rind or washed rind) might include Milleens, Cooleeney, or Durrus; a semi-firm flight (cooked and uncooked pressed cheeses) could

include waxed-rind varieties like Blarney Swiss, Carrigaline, or Coolea. If you know your guests are partial to Cheddars, goat cheeses, or blues, arrange a flight that features only these varieties. Sample cheeses in sequence from soft to hard and mild to strong, and choose wines that complement the cheeses being served.

The general guidelines are to match hearty red wines with robust cheeses and white wines with more delicate ones. Otherwise, classic match-ups are soft and semisoft cheeses with light-bodied wines like Beaujolais, Pinot Noir, Côtes de Beaune, and Chardonnay; semifirm Cheddars and Gouda-style cheeses with fruity white wines such as Riesling and Gewürztraminer or medium-bodied red wines such as Côtes du Rhône, Cabernet Sauvignon, and Merlot; blues with full-bodied reds like Burgundy, sweet dessert wines, sparkling wines, and port; goat and sheep cheeses with medium-bodied Zinfandel, French Sancerre, Chablis, or Sauvignon Blanc.

The essential accompaniment to wine and cheese is fresh, simple, crusty bread. The most typical accompani-

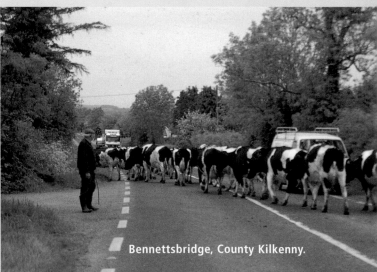

Bennettsbridge, County Kilkenny.

ment, though, is fruit, because of the contrast it provides to cheese, like a soft pear with an earthy Durrus, a crisp apple with a salty-sweet Cashel Blue, or a ripe fig with a tangy goat cheese like Corleggy. The sweet, tangy flavor of chutney matches well with the drier and more tart cheeses, like mature Coolea with Apple-Pear Chutney, St. Tola goat cheese with Rhubarb and Orange Chutney, or Dubliner with Cranberry-Walnut Chutney (pages 32–33).

In England and Northern Europe, there's a tradition of complementing local cheeses with ciders, beers, and ales, so in place of wine, you might like to try a good yeasty Irish beer in a washed-rind flight, a sweet cider in a goat cheese flight, or Guinness in a flight of mature blues. A light lager goes well in a flight that includes Blarney Castle or Kerrygold Swiss, and an ale in a flight with Vintage Cheddar or Dubliner.

For a complete list of Irish cheese varieties, see "An Irish Cheese Board" (pages 16–17). See Resources (page 161) for details on where to buy Irish cheese and Irish-made chutneys.

West Cork Food Fair.

Mannings Emporium, Ballylickey, County Cork.

Ireland's clean and unpolluted countryside makes it a perfect haven for food foraging, especially for mushrooms, of which it has approximately one hundred edible species. No need for the average cook to forage, however, thanks to the increased availability of wild, or "specialty," mushrooms (most often farm-grown) in the market today: chanterelles, porcini, morels, portobello, crimini (baby portobello), shiitakes, oysters, and enoki. These are particularly popular and appear regularly in dishes like these miniature "puffs," made with Irish Cheddar or Swiss cheeses.

WILD MUSHROOM CHEESE PUFFS

2 tablespoons olive oil

4 ounces mixed wild mushrooms, finely chopped

1 tablespoon minced shallot

3 eggs

⅔ cup half-and-half

1 tablespoon minced fresh flat-leaf parsley

½ teaspoon dry mustard

Salt and freshly ground pepper to taste

¼ cup fresh seasoned bread crumbs (recipe follows)

1 cup (4 ounces) shredded Swiss or Cheddar cheese, preferably Kerrygold brand

Preheat the oven to 350°F. Generously grease 24 miniature muffin cups.

In a large skillet over medium heat, heat the olive oil. Add the mushrooms and shallot and sauté for 3 to 5 minutes, or until soft. Evenly distribute the mushrooms among the muffin cups.

In a large bowl, whisk the eggs, half-and-half, parsley, mustard, salt, pepper, and bread crumbs together. Stir in the cheese. Spoon the egg mixture into the muffin cups and bake for 25 to 30 minutes, or until lightly browned and puffed. Remove from the oven and let cool for 5 minutes. Loosen with a knife and transfer to a serving plate. Serve now, or let cool and reheat puffs in a preheated 300°F oven for 5 minutes.

MAKES 24 PUFFS

Seasoned Bread Crumbs

Cut 5 to 6 slices stale baguette into ½-inch cubes. Place in a blender, or food processor fitted with a grating attachment. Add 1 teaspoon dried parsley, ¼ teaspoon dried basil, ¼ teaspoon dried oregano, and salt and freshly ground pepper to taste. Process for 15 to 20 seconds, or until the mixture is ground into fine crumbs.

MAKES ABOUT 1 CUP

Bunratty Folk Park, County Clare.

Crackers and cheese, cheese and wine, cheese and fruit: dynamic duos for any party, Irish or otherwise. In Ireland, though, cheese rarely comes to the table without the accompaniment of a good chutney or relish made with autumn fruits or summer vegetables. And while there are a number of very good home-style, commercially made chutneys available, they're simple to make yourself. Chef Joe Ryan of the Park Hotel Kenmare combines rhubarb and oranges in his recipe, while chef Noel McMeel of Castle Leslie in County Monaghan salutes autumn in a harvest blend of apples and pears. Another favorite combines cranberries, dates, apples, and walnuts. Try one of these on a cheese board, with a warm goat cheese salad, with pâté and toasted brioche, or with cold or smoked meat.

CHUTNEYS FOR CHEESE

Rhubarb and Orange Chutney

2 Valencia oranges

1½ pounds rhubarb, cut into 1-inch lengths

1 large onion, chopped

½ cup golden raisins

½ cup dark raisins

1½ cups malt vinegar

1½ cups packed brown sugar

½ teaspoon ground mace

½ teaspoon ground cinnamon

½ teaspoon ground allspice

Cut off the top and bottom of each orange down to the flesh. Stand each orange on end and cut off the peel down to the flesh. Seed the oranges and cut them into small pieces, reserving the juice. In a large nonreactive saucepan, combine the oranges, juice, and all the remaining ingredients. Bring to a boil, then reduce heat to a simmer and cook for 2 to 2½ hours, or until the mixture is thick and dark. Stir frequently to prevent sticking.

Let cool to room temperature. Cover and refrigerate for up to 2 weeks. Serve at room temperature.

MAKES 6 CUPS

Apple-Pear Chutney

⅓ cup chopped onion

⅓ cup cider vinegar

1 teaspoon minced fresh ginger

1 cup packed brown sugar

¾ cup golden raisins

1½ cups diced apples

1½ cups diced pears

In a large, nonreactive saucepan, combine all the ingredients. Bring to a boil, then reduce heat to medium-low and cook, uncovered, for 20 to 25 minutes, or until thickened. Let cool to room temperature. Cover and refrigerate for up to 2 weeks. Serve at room temperature.

MAKES 1½ CUPS

Cranberry-Walnut Chutney

1½ cups cranberries

⅔ cup packed brown sugar

½ cup chopped dates

⅓ cup chopped celery

⅓ cup diced apple

1 tablespoon chopped candied ginger

1 tablespoon fresh lemon juice

½ onion, finely chopped

¼ cup water

¼ cup chopped walnuts

In a large, nonreactive saucepan, combine all the ingredients. Bring to a boil, then reduce heat to medium-low and cook, uncovered, for 20 to 25 minutes, or until thickened. Let cool to room temperature. Cover and refrigerate for up to 2 weeks. Serve at room temperature.

MAKES 1½ CUPS

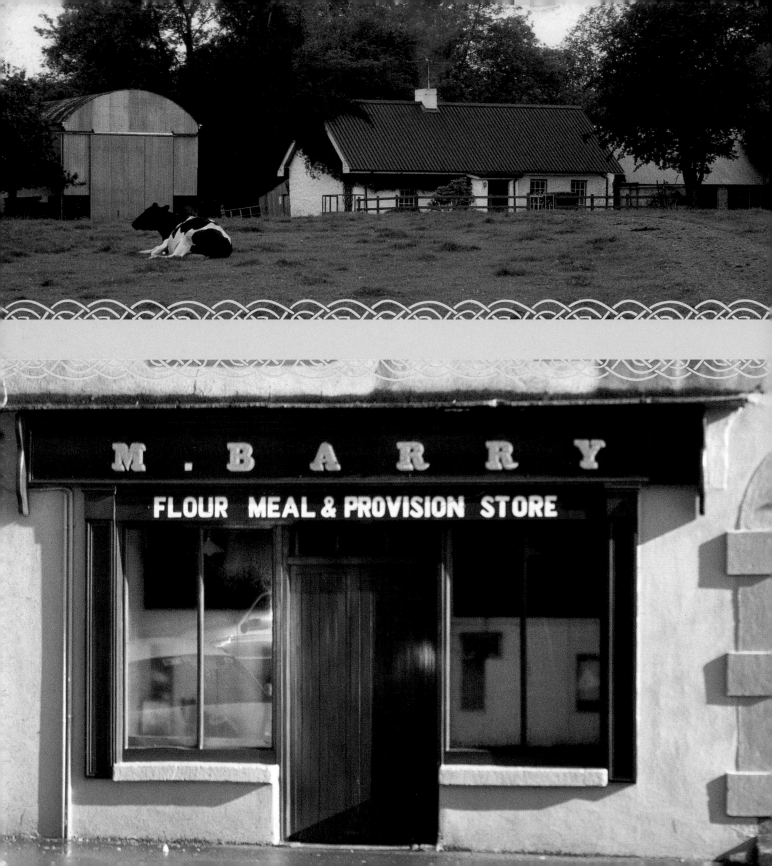

STARTERS

Opposite, top: Belturbet, County Cavan. Opposite, bottom: Gort, County Galway.

Brotchán foltchep (from the Irish words meaning "broth" and "leeks") is a traditional leek and oatmeal soup that has been served in Ireland for generations. Today, most cooks thicken the leek broth with potatoes instead of oatmeal. This soup can be altered from homespun to modern by swirling tangy buttermilk into it, topping it with a dollop of crème fraîche, or adding spices. It may also be used as a base for other potato soups made with cabbage, turnips, or seafood (variations follow).

POTATO AND LEEK SOUP

4 tablespoons unsalted butter

2 pounds potatoes, peeled and sliced

1 large leek (about 1 pound), white and light green parts only, washed and sliced

1 onion, chopped

1 stalk celery, chopped

5 cups homemade chicken stock or canned low-salt chicken broth

2½ cups milk

1 bay leaf

2 tablespoons minced fresh flat-leaf parsley

Salt and ground white pepper to taste

½ cup buttermilk or half-and-half

¼ cup minced fresh chives

In a large soup pot, melt the butter over medium heat. Add the vegetables, cover, and cook for 5 to 7 minutes, stirring frequently. Add the stock or broth, ½ cup of the milk, the bay leaf, parsley, salt, and pepper. Reduce heat to low, cover, and cook for 25 to 30 minutes, or until the vegetables are tender. Remove from heat.

Discard the bay leaf and let the soup let cool for 10 to 15 minutes. Transfer to a food processor or blender in batches and process until smooth. (To make ahead, cover and refrigerate for up to 12 hours.)

Return the purée to the soup pot. Stir in the remaining 2 cups milk. Cook over medium heat and heat through. Ladle the soup into bowls, swirl 1 tablespoon half-and-half or buttermilk into each serving, and sprinkle with the chives.

SERVES 8

SPRING CABBAGE SOUP: Add 2 cups shredded cabbage to the vegetables and a pinch of ground nutmeg.

SILKY TURNIP SOUP: Substitute 1 pound turnips, peeled and diced, for the leeks, and ¼ cup minced fresh parsley for the chives, and add a pinch of ground nutmeg.

POTATO-LEEK SOUP WITH SEAFOOD: Sauté 8 ounces shelled and deveined medium shrimp and 6 coarsely chopped sea scallops in 1 tablespoon unsalted butter over medium-high heat for 3 to 4 minutes, or until the shrimp turn pink. Divide the seafood among bowls of soup.

Bewleys Café on Grafton Street, Dublin, is a favorite spot for shoppers and nearby Trinity College students, who can linger there undisturbed for hours over a pot of tea, a cup of coffee, or a bowl of soup. Although the building has been modernized and lighter fare added to the menu, soups like this hearty parsnip and apple remain a favorite.

ROASTED PARSNIP, APPLE, AND GINGER SOUP

3 large parsnips (about 1½ pounds), peeled and thickly sliced

2 Granny Smith apples (about 1 pound), peeled, cored, and coarsely chopped

1 teaspoon minced peeled fresh ginger

Olive oil for coating

2 tablespoons unsalted butter

1 large leek (about 1 pound), white and light green parts only, washed and sliced

4 stalks celery, finely chopped

1 onion, chopped

1½ pounds potatoes, peeled and cut into ½-inch pieces

8 cups homemade chicken stock or canned low-salt chicken broth

½ cup half-and-half

Salt and freshly ground pepper to taste

Crème fraîche for garnish (page 105)

Parsnip Crisps for garnish (recipe follows), optional

Preheat the oven to 350°F. In an ovenproof casserole dish, combine the parsnips, apples, and ginger. Add oil, toss to coat, cover, and cook for 20 minutes. Stir, then cook, uncovered, for 20 minutes, or until the vegetables are lightly browned and tender.

In a large soup pot, melt the butter over medium heat. Add the leek, celery, onion, and potatoes. Cook for 4 to 5 minutes, or until slightly tender. Add the parsnip mixture and the stock or broth. Reduce heat to low, cover, and cook for 30 minutes, or until all the vegetables are soft. Let cool. Transfer to a blender or food processor in batches and process until smooth. (To make ahead, cover and refrigerate for up to 24 hours.)

Return the purée to the soup pot. Stir in the half-and-half and season with salt and pepper. Cook over medium

heat to heat through. Ladle the soup into bowls, put a spoonful of crème fraîche in the center, and sprinkle with parsnip crisps, if you wish.

SERVES 10 TO 12

Parsnip Crisps

Using a vegetable peeler, peel 1 large parsnip, then continue cutting into long, thin strips. Spread the strips out on a paper towel to dry slightly. In a large skillet, heat 2 tablespoons canola oil over medium heat. Fry the strips in batches for 2 to 3 minutes, or until they twist up and crisp. With a slotted spoon, transfer to paper towels to drain. Sprinkle with salt and pepper to taste.

Beth Hallinan, chef-owner of Rathcoursey House, Ballinacurra (near Midleton), County Cork, uses as many local ingredients as possible for her eighteenth-century Georgian-country-house meals. Some are cultivated in her garden, while others, like the nettles and ramps (wild onion) in this soup, are found wild in the surrounding countryside. Ms. Hallinan loves this green springtime soup for its interesting blend of flavors.

RATHCOURSEY EMERALD SOUP

4 tablespoons unsalted butter

½ onion, finely chopped

1 cup packed watercress sprigs, chopped

Leaves from 1 head butter lettuce, well rinsed and chopped

1 cup packed spinach leaves, chopped

2 handfuls young nettles or arugula (see note)

1 tablespoon chopped ramp leaves (wild onion) or garlic cloves (see note)

3 tablespoons flour

Grated zest of 1 lemon

4 cups homemade chicken stock or canned low-salt chicken broth

Salt and freshly ground pepper to taste

1⅔ cups half-and-half

Minced fresh chives or flat-leaf parsley for garnish

Garlic croutons for garnish (recipe follows), optional

In a large soup pot, melt the butter over medium heat. Add the onion and cook for 2 to 3 minutes, or until soft. Add the watercress, lettuce, spinach, nettles or arugula, and ramp leaves or garlic, and cook, stirring frequently, for 2 to 3 minutes, or until the vegetables are wilted.

Stir in the flour, lemon zest, stock or broth, salt, and pepper, and bring to a boil. Let cool. Transfer to a blender or food processor in batches and process until smooth. Return the purée to the soup pot. Stir in the half-and-half and cook over medium heat to heat through. Taste and adjust the seasoning.

Ladle the soup into bowls and sprinkle with chives or parsley. Top with a few garlic croutons, if you wish.

SERVES 6

NOTE: *If you want a stronger garlic flavor in your soup, cook 1 tablespoon minced garlic or 2 tablespoons chopped scallions with the onion. Nettles and ramps may be found in some farmers' markets and specialty produce markets in spring and early summer.*

Garlic Croutons

Remove the crusts from 3 to 4 slices white bread and cut into ½-inch cubes. In a large skillet, melt 4 tablespoons butter over medium heat. Add ½ teaspoon minced garlic and the bread cubes. Sauté until golden brown. Drain on paper towels and season with salt and pepper to taste. For added crispness, place on a baking sheet and bake in a preheated 250°F oven for about 15 minutes.

MAKES ABOUT 1¼ CUPS

For centuries, salmon has been smoked in Ireland using time-honored techniques that capture and enhance the flavor and texture of this great fish. The recipe for chowder, an anglicization of *chaudière,* the French word for the large iron cauldron fishermen used to make their soups, is a perfect way to make a little smoked salmon go a long way. It's perfect as a starter, or for lunch with a salad and brown soda bread.

SMOKED SALMON CHOWDER

2 tablespoons unsalted butter

1 onion, chopped

1 clove garlic, minced

4 ounces white mushrooms, chopped

2 tablespoons minced fresh flat-leaf parsley

4 ounces smoked salmon, chopped

Ground white pepper to taste

¼ cup all-purpose flour

2 cups homemade fish stock (recipe follows) or bottled clam juice

½ cup half-and-half

Crème fraîche for garnish (page 105)

4 dill sprigs for garnish

In a medium saucepan, melt the butter over medium heat. Add the onion, garlic, mushrooms, and parsley. Cook for 2 to 3 minutes, or until the vegetables are tender. Add the salmon and pepper and sauté for 2 minutes more, or until the salmon is heated through.

Remove from the heat and stir in the flour. Gradually stir in the fish stock or clam juice. Return to medium heat and bring to a boil. Reduce heat to a simmer and cook for 2 to 3 minutes, or until thickened. Stir in the half-and-half.

To serve, ladle into bowls. Put a spoonful of crème fraîche and a dill sprig in the center of each serving.

SERVES 4

Fish Stock

In a large saucepan, melt 2 tablespoons unsalted butter over medium heat. Add 1 chopped carrot and 1 chopped onion, and cook for 3 to 5 minutes, or until tender. Stir in 1¼ cups dry white wine and cook for 5 minutes, or until reduced by half. Add 2 to 3 pounds fish trimmings (heads, bones, skin), 3 to 4 sprigs fresh flat-leaf parsley, 8 to 10 peppercorns, a pinch of salt, 1 bay leaf, and 5 cups water. Bring to a boil, then reduce heat to a simmer and cook for 25 to 30 minutes, skimming frequently. Remove from heat, and let cool. Strain through muslin or a fine sieve. Can refrigerate for up to 2 days, or freeze for up to 2 months.

MAKES ABOUT 6 CUPS

Sautéed mushrooms and fried black pudding make an interesting combination in this recipe from chef Marie Harding of Lovett's Restaurant, Douglas, County Cork. She tops it with a slightly sweetened vinaigrette, the house recipe.

WILD MUSHROOM AND BLACK PUDDING SALAD

LOVETT'S VINAIGRETTE:

½ cup sunflower oil

½ cup white wine vinegar

2 heaping teaspoons Dijon mustard

1 teaspoon sugar

½ teaspoon minced garlic

1 teaspoon minced shallot

Salt and freshly ground pepper to taste

SALAD:

2 tablespoons olive oil

12 slices black pudding, preferably Galtee brand

4 tablespoons unsalted butter

1 tablespoon chopped green onion or fresh chives

1 tablespoon minced shallot

8 ounces mixed wild mushrooms, such as oysters, chanterelles, and stemmed shiitakes, coarsely chopped

1 teaspoon fresh lemon juice

Salt and freshly ground pepper to taste

10 ounces mixed salad greens

TO MAKE THE VINAIGRETTE: Combine all the vinaigrette ingredients in a small jar, cover, and shake until blended. Refrigerate until ready to use.

TO MAKE THE SALAD: In a large skillet over medium heat, heat the olive oil. Fry the pudding slices for 3 to 5 minutes on each side, or until browned. Using a slotted metal spatula, transfer to paper towels to drain.

In another large skillet, melt the butter over medium heat. Add the green onion or chives, shallot, and mushrooms, and sauté for 3 to 4 minutes, or until the vegetables are tender. Stir in the lemon juice and season with salt and pepper.

To serve, in a large salad bowl, toss the greens with the vinaigrette. Divide among 4 salad plates. Place 3 slices of pudding on each salad and spoon the warm mushrooms and juices over the top.

SERVES 4

With so many wonderful goat cheeses being crafted in Ireland today (Corbetstown, Corleggy, Croghan, St. Tola, Oisin, and Poulcoin are some to look for), it's no surprise to find the tangy cheese the French call *chèvre* turning up in so many recipes. Here, it's made into lightly breaded "fritters" and served atop a mix of fresh greens. The flavor of the cheese is nicely complemented by the mustard seed dressing.

GARDEN GREENS WITH GOAT CHEESE FRITTERS

MUSTARD SEED DRESSING:

1½ teaspoons whole-grain mustard, preferably Lakeshore brand

½ teaspoon packed brown sugar

¼ teaspoon honey

1 cup olive oil

1 tablespoon tarragon vinegar

FRITTERS:

1 cup fresh seasoned bread crumbs (page 30)

¼ cup all-purpose flour

1 egg

1 tablespoon milk

3 logs (4 ounces each) fresh white goat cheese, preferably Irish

1½ cups canola oil

10 ounces mixed salad greens

½ cup dried cranberries

Freshly ground pepper to taste

TO MAKE THE DRESSING: Combine all the ingredients in a small jar, cover, and shake until blended. Refrigerate until ready to use.

TO MAKE THE FRITTERS: Put the bread crumbs and flour on separate plates. In a small bowl, lightly beat the egg and milk. Cut the cheese into 12 pieces. Flour your hands, roll the cheese into balls, then flatten slightly. Roll each ball in the flour and dip in the egg mixture, then the bread crumbs. Gently pat the crumbs into the cheese and refrigerate for 15 minutes.

In a large skillet, heat the oil over medium heat. Cook the fritters, 3 to 4 at a time, for 1 minute on each side, or until golden brown. Using a slotted spoon, transfer to paper towels to drain.

In a large bowl, toss the greens with the vinaigrette. Divide among 4 salad plates. Place 3 fritters on each plate and sprinkle the dried cranberries over the greens. Top with a few grinds of pepper.

SERVES 4

Hazel Bourke, chef-owner with her husband, Joe, of Assolas House, Kanturk, County Cork, is one of Ireland's most respected chefs. In 1999, she was a finalist in Wedgwood China's prestigious Chef and Potter Competition with this entry featuring local mussels and tiny new potatoes from her garden.

WARM POTATO SALAD WITH KENMARE BAY MUSSELS

ASSOLAS HOUSE VINAIGRETTE:

2 shallots, minced

1 tablespoon minced garlic

1 tablespoon Dijon mustard

2 tablespoons tarragon vinegar

¼ cup olive oil

½ cup sunflower oil

2 tablespoons minced fresh herbs, such as tarrragon, chives, and/or chervil

Salt and freshly ground pepper to taste

SALAD:

1 pound new potatoes

2 pounds mussels, scrubbed and debearded

¼ cup dry white wine

10 ounces mixed salad greens

TO MAKE THE VINAIGRETTE: In a blender or food processor, combine the shallots, garlic, mustard, and tarragon vinegar. Process for 10 to 15 seconds, or until smooth. With the machine running, gradually add in the olive oil and sunflower oil, and process for 10 seconds, or until well blended. Transfer to a small jar, add the herbs, salt, and pepper, cover, and shake until blended. Refrigerate until ready to use.

TO MAKE THE SALAD: Cook the potatoes in salted boiling water for 12 to 15 minutes, or until tender. Drain and let cool for 5 minutes. Transfer to a large bowl and toss with half the vinaigrette dressing. Let stand at room temperature for 2 hours.

Put the mussels in a large saucepan with 1 cup water. Set it over medium heat, cover, and cook for 6 to 8 minutes, or until the shells open. With a slotted spoon, transfer the mussels to a large bowl. Remove the mussels from the shells. Discard any that have not opened.

In a large saucepan, heat the wine over medium heat. Add the potatoes and mussels and cook for 3 to 5 minutes, or until heated through.

To serve, divide the lettuce among 6 salad plates, spoon the potatoes and mussels over, and drizzle with the remaining vinaigrette.

SERVES 6

Celebrating Seafood
Oyster Festivals in Galway and Clarenbridge; Mussel Fair in Bantry

The Irish are celebratory when it comes to food, especially the first oysters of the season in September, after their long nap through months without an "r," and mussels in May, when the crop is harvested.

Clarenbridge, County Galway.

Two locations in County Galway—Clarenbridge and Galway City—host food fests that honor the oyster in three-day extravaganzas that include shucking contests and black-tie balls. The residents of Clarenbridge (nine miles south of Galway), who proclaim "the world is your oyster and Clarenbridge its home," have held their festival on the second weekend of September since 1954. Since native (not farm-raised) oysters are not eaten during the summer months, their reentry, or "wake-up call" as the residents of Clarenbridge call it, is celebrated with a weekend of *craic* (Irish for "good times"). While most of the events—cooking demonstrations, oyster opening competitions, seafood luncheons—are held under a festival marquee around Paddy Burke's pub, the festivities spread to the pubs and restaurants throughout the village, Moran's, Raftery's Rest, O'Donaghue's, Sherry's, and Jordan's bars among them. The traditional accompaniment is Murphy's Stout, the main sponsor.

Also founded in 1954, the Galway International Oyster Festival takes place on the last weekend of September, undoubtedly to allow a sufficient time for locals to recuperate from the Clarenbridge bash. The word *Guinness* precedes the name of most events, since the sponsor hosts many of them, including the international oyster-opening championship that draws aficionados from all over the world. Guinness also supplies libations at events held under the festival marquee pitched at the historic Spanish Arch and along the pub trail throughout the city. Music, parades, an "elegant lady" competition, receptions, brunches, and balls add to the general revelry.

In Bantry, Country Cork, it's Mussels and Murphy's (a Cork-brewed stout) nonstop over the first weekend of May, when a similar weekend of partying pays homage to the local shellfish. For details, see Resources (page 161).

Roundstone, County Galway.

Chef Robbie Millar and his wife, Shirley, are the affable hosts of Shanks, a Sir Terence Conran–designed restaurant at the Blackwood Golf Club, Bangor, County Down. One of Ireland's most respected chefs, Millar loves to give Irish classics a new twist. Here, smoky bacon, creamy lentils, and walnut oil give smoked haddock an autumn kick.

SMOKED HADDOCK AND BACON SALAD

SHANKS VINAIGRETTE:

1 cup olive oil

¼ cup walnut oil

¼ cup red wine vinegar

Salt and freshly ground pepper to taste

SALAD:

⅓ cup dried lentils

1 carrot, peeled and cut into 2-inch pieces

1 leek, white part only, rinsed and quartered

1 small onion, quartered

1 clove garlic

8 cups water

⅔ cup milk

12 ounces smoked haddock fillet

2 tablespoons prepared horseradish

½ cup heavy cream

Salt and freshly ground pepper to taste

1 tablespoon canola oil

8 ounces traditional Irish bacon or Canadian bacon, chopped

2 tablespoons minced fresh chives

10 ounces mixed salad greens

TO MAKE THE VINAIGRETTE: Combine all the ingredients in a small jar, cover, and shake until blended. Refrigerate until ready to use.

TO MAKE THE SALAD: In a large saucepan, combine the lentils, carrot, leek, onion, and garlic. Add the water, bring to a boil, then reduce heat to simmer and cook for 40 minutes, or until the lentils are tender. Drain the lentils and discard the vegetables.

In a large skillet, heat the milk over medium heat and poach the haddock for 2 to 3 minutes, or until heated through. Using a slotted spoon, transfer the haddock to a plate and keep warm. Drizzle with a little vinaigrette. Pour off half the milk.

Add the horseradish and cream to the milk in the pan and cook for 3 to 5 minutes, or until thickened. Strain into a small saucepan and season with salt and pepper. Stir in the lentils. Set aside and keep warm.

In a large skillet, heat the oil over medium heat. Cook the bacon until crisp.

To serve, divide the greens among 4 salad plates and drizzle with the vinaigrette. Cut the haddock into slices and arrange over the greens. Sprinkle the bacon and chives over the top, and spoon the creamed lentils around the greens.

SERVES 4

McDonagh's Seafood, Quay Street, Galway City.

I first tasted a "twice-baked" soufflé at Rathmullan House, an early-nineteenth-century country house on the shore of Lough Swilly in beautiful County Donegal. Donegal is sometimes called the "forgotten county" for its wild, remote location in the northwest corner of Ireland, but a stay at Rathmullan, along with the food served there, is cause for fond remembrance. When I asked for this recipe, Rathmullan hostess Robin Wheeler gladly obliged, noting that given their location by the sea, a seafood recipe would be a perfect example of their cooking style as well as being "simple and foolproof."

TWICE-BAKED CRABMEAT SOUFFLÉS

RATHMULLAN DIJON VINAIGRETTE:

½ cup olive oil

¼ cup red wine vinegar

½ teaspoon salt

¼ teaspoon freshly ground pepper

2 tablespoons Dijon mustard

SOUFFLÉS:

⅔ cup milk

1 slice onion

Pinch of ground nutmeg

3 tablespoons unsalted butter

½ cup all-purpose flour

Pinch of dry mustard

6 ounces fresh lump crabmeat, picked over for shell

Salt and freshly ground pepper to taste

2 egg yolks

4 egg whites

Fresh seasoned bread crumbs (page 30) for dusting

10 ounces mixed salad greens

Parsley sprigs for garnish

TO MAKE THE VINAIGRETTE: Combine all the ingredients in a small jar, cover, and shake until blended. Refrigerate until ready to use.

TO MAKE THE SOUFFLÉS: Preheat the oven to 350°F. Butter six 6-ounce ramekins and line the bottoms of each with a round of waxed paper.

In a small saucepan, combine the milk, onion, and nutmeg. Bring to a boil over medium heat. In a medium saucepan, melt the butter over medium heat. Add the flour and mustard and cook for 2 minutes, whisking constantly. Gradually whisk in the hot milk. Cook for about 5 minutes, or until thick, whisking constantly. Add the crabmeat, salt, and pepper.

In a small bowl, whisk the egg yolks, then stir them into the soufflé mixture. Remove from the heat and let cool.

In a large bowl, beat the egg whites until stiff, glossy peaks form. Mix one-fourth of the whites into the soufflé mixture to lighten it. Fold in the remaining whites.

Dust the ramekins with the bread crumbs and shake out the excess. Spoon the soufflé mixture into the ramekins and place in a baking pan. Add enough hot water to the baking pan to come halfway up the side of the dishes. Bake for 20 to 25 minutes, or until puffed, browned, and set in the center. Remove the baking pan from the oven and let the soufflés cool in the pan for 15 minutes. Run a sharp knife around the side of the ramekins to loosen the soufflés, then lift them out onto a buttered baking sheet. Refrigerate for up to 4 hours.

To serve, reheat the soufflés on the baking sheet in a preheated 350°F oven for about 10 minutes, or until heated through. Divide the greens among 6 salad plates and drizzle with the vinaigrette. Place a soufflé in the center of each salad and top with parsley.

SERVES 6

Savory soufflés are gaining popularity throughout Ireland as a starter, served alone atop a well-dressed salad or accompanied with other ingredients as in this recipe. Ian Connolly, chef-owner of Moe's Restaurant, Dublin, adds a double dose of apple punch here with an apple purée and a cider vinaigrette. Chunky applesauce can be substituted for the apple purée.

CASHEL BLUE SOUFFLÉS WITH BLACK PUDDING AND APPLE CIDER PURÉE

MOE'S CIDER VINAIGRETTE:

½ cup olive oil

¼ cup cider vinegar

½ teaspoon salt

¼ teaspoon freshly ground pepper

CASHEL BLUE SOUFFLÉS:

⅔ cup milk

3 tablespoons unsalted butter

½ cup all-purpose flour

6 ounces Cashel Blue cheese or other blue cheese, cut into small pieces

Salt and freshly ground pepper to taste

2 egg yolks

4 egg whites

2 tablespoons ground hazelnuts or walnuts for dusting

2 tablespoons olive oil

12 slices black pudding, preferably Galtee brand, thinly sliced

APPLE CIDER PURÉE:

1 large Granny Smith apple, peeled, cored, and sliced

About ¾ cup apple cider

Salt and freshly ground pepper to taste

Sugar to taste

5 ounces mixed arugula and spinach leaves

TO MAKE THE VINAIGRETTE: Combine all the ingredients in a small jar, cover, and shake until blended. Refrigerate until ready to use.

TO MAKE THE SOUFFLÉS: Preheat the oven to 350°F. Butter four 6-ounce ramekins and line the bottoms with a round of waxed paper.

In a small saucepan, bring the milk to a simmer over medium heat. Set aside. In a medium saucepan, melt the butter over medium heat. Add the flour and cook for 2 minutes, whisking constantly. Gradually whisk in the hot milk. Cook for about 5 minutes, or until thick, whisking constantly. Add the cheese and stir until smooth. Stir in the salt and pepper. Whisk the egg yolks in a small bowl, then stir into the soufflé mixture. Remove from the heat and let cool for 5 minutes.

In a large bowl, beat the egg whites until stiff, glossy peaks form. Stir one-fourth of the whites into the soufflé mixture to lighten it. Fold in the remaining whites.

Dust the ramekins with the ground nuts and shake out the excess. Spoon the soufflé mixture into the ramekins and place in a baking pan. Add enough hot water to the baking pan to come halfway up the side of the dishes. Bake for 20 to 25 minutes, or until the soufflés are puffed, browned, and set in the center. Remove the baking pan from the oven and let the soufflés cool in the pan for 15 minutes.

In a large skillet, heat the olive oil over medium heat. Cook the pudding slices for 3 to 5 minutes on each side, or until browned.

TO MAKE THE APPLE PURÉE: Put the apple slices in a small saucepan and add cider to barely cover. Cook over medium-low heat for 10 to 15 minutes, or until the cider has evaporated and the apples are soft. Season with salt and pepper and sprinkle with sugar. Mash the apples with a fork.

To serve, put the arugula and spinach in a large bowl and toss with the vinaigrette. Divide the greens among 4 salad plates. Run a sharp knife around the side of the ramekins to loosen the soufflés, then lift out and place one in the center of each salad. Place 3 spoonfuls of apple purée around each and put a slice of pudding on top of each spoonful of pureé.

SERVES 4

This simple but innovative dish from chef Marie Harding of Lovett's Restaurant, Douglas, County Cork, takes one of Ireland's best-known dishes, made of mashed potatoes and known as champ, and transforms it into a tasty and sophisticated starter.

CRAB AND CHAMP BAKE WITH TOMATO-WATERCRESS DRESSING

TOMATO-WATERCRESS DRESSING:

1 tomato, peeled, seeded, and diced

½ bunch watercress, rinsed, stemmed, and coarsely chopped

¼ cup olive oil

1 teaspoon Lakeshore or other whole-grain mustard

1 teaspoon sugar

¼ cup cider vinegar

Salt and freshly ground pepper to taste

CHAMP:

2 pounds potatoes, peeled and cut into ½-inch pieces

4 tablespoons unsalted butter

4 tablespoons minced fresh chives

Salt and freshly ground pepper to taste

Dash of ground nutmeg

CRAB FILLING:

1¼ cups heavy cream

½ cup homemade fish stock (page 40) or bottled clam juice

¼ teaspoon grated lemon zest

1 tablespoon flour

8 ounces fresh lump crabmeat, picked over for shell

Salt and freshly ground pepper to taste

Dash of Tabasco sauce

½ cup (2 ounces) shredded smoked Gubbeen cheese or other smoked cheese

TO MAKE THE DRESSING: Combine all the ingredients in a large bowl and stir with a fork to blend. Cover and refrigerate until ready to use.

TO MAKE THE CHAMP: Cook the potatoes in salted boiling water for 12 to 15 minutes, or until tender. Drain and mash.

Meanwhile, in a small skillet, melt the butter over medium heat. Add the chives and cook for 1 to 2 minutes, or until soft. Add to the mashed potatoes and season with salt, pepper, and nutmeg. Set aside.

TO MAKE THE CRAB FILLING: In a small saucepan, whisk the cream, fish stock or clam juice, lemon zest, and flour together and cook over medium heat for 2 to 3 minutes, or until thickened. Remove from the heat, stir in the crabmeat, and season with salt, pepper, and Tabasco sauce.

Preheat the oven to 400°F. Butter four 6-ounce ramekins and put them on a baking sheet. Spoon the champ into the ramekins. Spoon the crab filling over the top.

Bake for 15 minutes, or until the filling is set.

Preheat the boiler. Sprinkle the crab and champ mixtures with the grated cheese, then place under the broiler 4 inches from the heat source and cook for about 2 minutes, or until the tops brown and the cheese bubbles.

To serve, run a sharp knife around the side of the ramekins to loosen, then lift out and put one of the crab and champ bakes in the center of each of 4 salad plates. Drizzle some of the dressing around and pass the remaining dressing in a bowl.

SERVES 4

Rock of Cashel, County Tipperary.

Creagh Gardens, near Skibbereen, County Cork.

Vegetarian dishes are growing in popularity in Ireland, along with the reputation of Denis Cotter, one of the first chefs to open a vegetarian restaurant, Café Paradiso, in Cork City. He features the "heroes of the season"—vegetables that are at the peak of their seasonal flavor—like late-summer beefsteak tomatoes, which star in this richly textured "charlotte" served on wilted greens. If you like, serve them "twice-baked" (see page 49).

GOAT CHEESE AND ROASTED TOMATO CHARLOTTE

FILLING:

Olive oil for brushing

6 beefsteak tomatoes

6 cloves garlic, minced

16 ounces fresh white goat cheese, preferably Oisin Farmhouse goat cheese, at room temperature

8 ounces cream cheese at room temperature

2 eggs

3 egg whites

1/3 to 1/2 cup half-and-half

1 tablespoon pine nuts

4 to 5 fresh basil leaves, chopped

Freshly ground pepper to taste

WILTED GREENS:

2 tablespoons olive oil

1 red onion, sliced

1 bunch fresh spinach, stemmed, chopped, and rinsed but not dried

Salt and freshly ground pepper to taste

TO MAKE THE FILLING: Preheat the oven to 250°F. Lightly brush 2 baking sheets with olive oil.

Cut each tomato horizontally into 3 thick slices. Place on the prepared pans, brush with olive oil, and roast, turning once, for about 1 hour, or until partly dried and slightly caramelized.

Increase the oven temperature to 375°F. Butter six 8-ounce ramekins and line the bottom of each with a round of waxed paper.

Meanwhile, in a food processor, combine the garlic, goat cheese, cream cheese, and whole eggs. Process for 1 to 2 minutes, or until smooth. With the machine running, add the egg whites, one at a time, then process for 30 seconds, or until well blended. Transfer the mixture to a medium bowl and stir in enough half-and-half to give it a thick pouring consistency. Stir in the pine nuts, basil, and pepper.

Put a tomato slice in each prepared ramekin, then spoon in 1 tablespoon of the cheese mixture. Repeat the process twice to make 3 layers in each ramekin. Place the ramekins in a baking pan. Add enough hot water to come halfway up the side of the dishes. Bake for 35 to 40 minutes, or until puffed, browned, and set in the center.

Remove the baking pan from the oven and let the charlottes sit in the pan for 5 minutes. Run a sharp knife around the side of the ramekins to loosen the charlottes.

TO MAKE THE WILTED GREENS: In a large skillet, heat the olive oil over medium heat. Add the onion and sauté for about 1 minute, then add the spinach and sauté, stirring constantly for 1 to 2 minutes, or until the greens are wilted. Season with salt and pepper. Divide among 6 salad plates, invert the charlottes onto the greens, and serve immediately.

SERVES 6

Crackpots, Carole Norman's restaurant and pottery studio, is in Kinsale, County Cork, the town considered Ireland's gourmet capital. A potter by trade and restaurateur by devotion, Norman serves meals at Crackpots on her hand-thrown pottery, which diners can also buy there. She's taken the concept of cheesecake to a new level by turning it into a savory starter and adding pickled pears. If you like, bake the cheesecakes in individual springform pans and serve them on mixed greens.

CASHEL BLUE CHEESECAKE WITH PICKLED PEARS

PICKLED PEARS:

⅔ cup olive oil

7 tablespoons balsamic vinegar

2 cloves garlic, minced

Salt and freshly ground pepper to taste

1 tablespoon mixed peppercorns

15 ounces canned pears, drained and sliced

BISCUIT BASE:

1¼ cups crumbs made from digestive biscuits such as McVitie's brand

½ cup ground walnuts

¾ cup (1½ sticks) unsalted butter, melted

FILLING:

1½ cups (6 ounces) Cashel Blue cheese or other blue cheese, cut into small pieces

6 eggs

Three 8-ounce packages cream cheese at room temperature

1 tablespoon minced fresh chives

1 tablespoon chopped green onions

Freshly ground pepper to taste

10 ounces mixed salad greens (optional)

TO MAKE THE PICKLED PEARS: In a jar, combine the olive oil, vinegar, garlic, salt, pepper, and peppercorns. Cover and shake until well blended. Put the pears in a glass bowl, pour the dressing over, cover, and refrigerate for at least 2 hours or up to 4 hours before serving.

TO MAKE THE BISCUIT BASE: Preheat the oven to 350°F. Lightly butter a 9-inch springform pan or eight 4-inch springform pans.

In a small bowl, combine the biscuit crumbs and walnuts. Add the butter and stir until until blended. Press into the bottom of the prepared pan(s) and bake for 8 to 10 minutes, or until firm and lightly browned. Remove from the oven and let cool for 20 minutes on a wire rack.

TO MAKE THE FILLING: Sprinkle the blue cheese over the biscuit base(s). In a food processor, combine the eggs, cream cheese, chives, and green onions. Process for 10 to 20 seconds, or until smooth. Season with pepper, spoon over the blue cheese and bake for 25 to 30 minutes, or until browned and set. Remove from the oven and let cool for 20 to 30 minutes on a wire rack. Remove the sides of the pan(s).

To serve, cut a large cheesecake into wedges and serve with 2 or 3 pear slices. Place each individual cheesecake in the center of a serving plate and surround with mixed greens, if you wish, and pear slices. Drizzle the greens with some of the pear marinade.

SERVES 8

Bunratty Folk Park, Bunratty, County Clare.

Seafood cakes, like these made with crabmeat, tarragon, and grated apple, make a great starter or light lunch. This recipe is an adaptation of several versions of crab cakes I've tasted in Ireland. Also try them with Creamy Whole-Grain Mustard Sauce (recipe follows).

CRAB CAKES WITH ROASTED RED PEPPER SAUCE

ROASTED RED PEPPER SAUCE:

One 7-ounce jar roasted red peppers, drained and chopped

1 cup mayonnaise

½ teaspoon Dijon mustard

2 tablespoons minced fresh flat-leaf parsley

2 tablespoons minced shallots

½ teaspoon fresh lemon juice

Salt and freshly ground pepper to taste

CRAB CAKES:

8 ounces fresh lump crabmeat, picked over for shell

1 egg

2 tablespoons mayonnaise

¼ cup finely chopped onion

½ Granny Smith apple, peeled, cored, and grated

1 tablespoon minced fresh flat-leaf parsley

1 teaspoon fresh tarragon

Dash of Tabasco sauce

¼ teaspoon cayenne pepper

Dash of Worcestershire sauce

Salt and freshly ground pepper to taste

1 tablespoon fresh lemon juice

1 to 2 cups fresh seasoned bread crumbs (page 30) for dredging

1 cup canola oil

TO MAKE THE SAUCE: In a food processsor, combine the peppers, mayonnaise, mustard, parsley, shallots, and lemon juice. Process for 1 to 2 minutes, or until smooth. Season with salt and pepper. Cover and refrigerate for up to 24 hours.

In a large bowl, combine all the crab cake ingredients except the bread crumbs and oil. Stir until well blended. Shape into 12 evenly sized cakes and dredge in the bread crumbs. Place on a baking sheet, cover with plastic wrap, and refrigerate for 2 hours.

In a large skillet, heat the oil over medium heat. Cook the crab cakes for 3 to 5 minutes on each side, or until golden brown. Serve immediately, or transfer to a baking sheet and keep warm in a low oven for 10 to 15 minutes. Serve the sauce alongside.

SERVES 12 AS A STARTER, 6 AS A LUNCH ENTRÉE

Creamy Whole-Grain Mustard Sauce

5 tablespoons unsalted butter

3 tablespoons minced shallots

2 tablespoons distilled white vinegar

⅓ cup dry white wine

½ cup heavy cream

2 tablespoons whole-grain mustard, preferably Lakeshore brand

Salt and freshly ground pepper to taste

In a small skillet, melt 1 tablespoon of the butter over medium-low heat. Add the shallots and sauté for 2 to 3 minutes, or until soft. Add the vinegar and cook for 1 minute. Add the wine and cook for 3 to 4 minutes, or until reduced to about ⅓ cup. Add the cream and cook 4 to 5 minutes, or until reduced to about ½ cup.

Remove from heat and whisk in the remaining 4 tablespoons butter. Strain through a fine-meshed sieve into a small bowl. Whisk in the mustard and season with salt and pepper. Cover and refrigerate for up to 24 hours.

MAKES ABOUT ¾ CUP

Guinness sabayon, a delectable hollandaise sauce flavored with Guinness stout, is delicious with oysters. This recipe from Derry Clarke, chef-owner of L'Ecrivain, Dublin, is an all-Irish adaptation of Oysters Rockefeller that substitutes bacon and cabbage for the usual spinach.

BAKED ROCK OYSTERS WITH BACON, CABBAGE, AND GUINNESS SABAYON

GUINNESS SABAYON:

2 egg yolks

½ cup Guinness stout

Dash of fresh lemon juice

Salt and freshly ground pepper to taste

1 cup (2 sticks) unsalted butter, melted

4 outer green cabbage leaves, finely shredded

1 teaspoon canola oil

4 slices traditional Irish bacon or Canadian bacon, chopped

24 oysters in the shell

TO MAKE THE SABAYON: In a double boiler, whisk the egg yolks, Guinness, lemon juice, salt, and pepper together. Place over barely simmering water and whisk for 3 to 5 minutes, or until the sauce begins to thicken. Remove from the heat and gradually drizzle in the melted butter until the sauce is well blended.

Cook the cabbage in salted boiling water for 1 to 2 minutes, or until slightly wilted. Drain and immerse in cold water. Drain again. In a small skillet, heat the oil over medium heat. Cook the bacon until crisp. Using a slotted spoon, transfer to paper towels to drain.

Preheat the broiler. Shuck the oysters over a small bowl. Reserve the deeper half of each shell and rinse them under cold water. Place the shells on a bed of rock salt in a small, sided baking sheet. Divide the cabbage among the shells, put an oyster on top of each, and sprinkle the bacon over the oysters. Spoon some of the sabayon over each. Place under the broiler 4 inches from the heat source and cook for about 3 minutes, or until the sauce is browned and bubbling. Serve immediately.

SERVES 4

NOTE: *To shuck oysters, insert the tip of a strong knife between the halves of the shell just behind the hinge or muscle. Cut through the muscle. Lift off the shallow shell. Loosen the oyster from the shell with the point of the knife.*

MAIN COURSES

Opposite, top: Carnlough, County Antrim. Opposite, bottom: Dublin.

This exotic-sounding dish is really quite simple to prepare. Created by head chef Tony Schwarz of the Mustard Seed at Echo Lodge, Ballingarry, County Limerick, it's just what a visitor would expect from one of Ireland's most-respected country houses. Under the supervision and ownership of Daniel Mullane, Echo Lodge was built in 1884 as a parochial house, was later a convent, and is now home to the Mustard Seed restaurant, which relocated from Adare in 1995. The house offers luxurious accommodations to complement its well-established dining room. Serve this dish with Colcannon (page 98) or Champ (page 101).

SALMON WITH LAND AND SEA VEGETABLES IN HERB BUTTER SAUCE

2 tablespoons dry white wine

½ cup fish stock (page 40) or bottled clam juice

Juice of ½ lemon

1 bay leaf

1 small carrot, sliced

½ red onion, chopped

1 small zucchini, chopped

4 cherry tomatoes, halved

1 cup packed spinach leaves, rinsed, and coarsely chopped

4 salmon fillets, skin and pin bones removed (5 to 6 ounces each)

½ cup (1 stick) unsalted butter, cut into small pieces

1 tablespoon minced fresh flat-leaf parsley

1 tablespoon minced fresh chives

½ teaspoon fennel seeds

Salt and freshly ground pepper to taste

4 strands *each* dried dulse, hijiki, and kombu, or 12 strands Ocean Greens sea vegetables

2 tablespoons canola oil

4 sprigs fennel for garnish

In a large nonreactive sauté pan or skillet, cook the white wine over medium heat until reduced by half. Add the fish stock or clam juice, lemon juice, bay leaf, and vegetables. Place the salmon on top. Cover and cook for 4 to 5 minutes, or until the vegetables are tender. With a slotted spoon, transfer the salmon to a plate and keep warm.

Stir in the butter, one piece at a time, until well blended. Stir in the herbs, salt, and pepper and cook for 30 seconds. Add the dulse and hijiki and cook for 1 minute. In a small skillet, heat the oil over medium heat. Quickly fry the kombu. Using a slotted spoon, transfer to paper towels to drain.

To serve, place a salmon fillet in the center of a plate, spoon the sauce and vegetables over, and garnish with the fried kombu and fennel sprigs.

SERVES 4

Cider is one of the oldest beverages known to man. If pairing it with fish seems an unlikely match, you'll be surprised at how perfectly they work together in this ultra-easy, one-step recipe from chef Frederic Souty of Kee's Hotel, Ballybofey, County Donegal. Given its location close to the sea and on the edge of the Blue Stack Mountains, seafood and mountain lamb predominate the menu at this long-established, family-run country hotel. Serve this dish with Carrot and Turnip Purée (page 111).

HADDOCK IN CIDER

2 tablespoons flour

Salt and freshly ground pepper to taste

4 haddock, cod, or whiting fillets (5 to 6 ounces each)

2 tablespoons minced shallots

1 tablespoon minced fresh flat-leaf parsley

Fennel or lemon thyme sprigs

4 slices lemon

1¼ cups Irish cider, preferably Magner's brand

1 tablespoon unsalted butter

Preheat the oven to 350°F. Butter an ovenproof baking dish.

In a shallow bowl, combine the flour, salt, and pepper. Dredge the fish in the seasoned flour. Place the floured fillets in the prepared dish and sprinkle with the shallots, parsley, and fennel or lemon thyme. Place the lemon slices on top, pour the cider over the fish, and dot with butter.

Cover with aluminum foil and bake for 20 to 25 minutes, or until the fish flakes and the sauce is bubbling.

Remove from the oven and preheat the broiler. Remove the foil and place the dish under the broiler 4 inches from the heat source for 1 to 2 minutes, or until lightly browned.

To serve, place a fish fillet in the center of each serving plate and spoon the sauce over the top.

SERVES 4

Salmon (Bradán)
Sea Trout (Breac muir)
John Dory (Deorai)
Black sole (Sól dubh)
Plaice (Leathóg)
Hake (Colmóir)
Lemon sole (Leathóg mhin)
Monk (Láimhineach)
Brill (Broit)

Dun Laoghaire, County Dublin.

This one-dish meal from chef David FitzGibbon of Aherne's Seafood Bar in Youghal, County Cork, features cod fillets cooked in packets with wine, fresh herbs, and wild mushrooms. Aherne's, which is also a guest house, has a decades-long reputation for serving the freshest local seafood, but the chef advises that this recipe is easy to adapt to whatever mild white fish is available. Serve with Accordion Potatoes (page 108).

COD IN A PARCEL

4 cod fillets (5 to 6 ounces each)

1 cup (2 ounces) wild mushrooms, chopped

¼ cup chopped leek

1 small stalk celery, julienned

1 small carrot, julienned

2 to 3 sprigs flat-leaf parsley

1 tablespoon minced fresh chives

¼ cup dry white wine

1 tablespoon Herb Butter (recipe follows)

Preheat the oven to 350°F. Line a large baking pan with aluminum foil and butter the foil.

Place the cod fillets in the prepared pan and cover with the mushrooms, leek, celery, carrot, and herbs. Pour the wine over the fish, dot with the herb butter, and wrap the fish in the foil, sealing the edges well. Cook for 20 to 25 minutes.

To serve, place a fish fillet in the center of each plate and spoon the sauce over the top.

SERVES 4

Herb Butter

In a small bowl, combine 4 tablespoons unsalted room-temperature butter with 1 clove shallot (minced), ½ tablespoon minced fresh chives, 1½ tablespoons minced fresh chervil, ¼ teaspoon salt, ¼ teaspoon ground pepper, and 1 teaspoon fresh lemon juice. Stir to blend. Refrigerate any leftover butter to use on grilled, broiled, or poached fish.

Seared scallops are hard to improve on, unless it's with a flavorful sauce, like this tomato-butter-leek sauce from chef-owner John Sheedy. With his wife, Martina, Sheedy recently took over the operation of his family's hotel, Sheedy's Country House, in Lisdoonvarna, County Clare. Serve this dish with Champ (page 101).

SAUCY SEARED SCALLOPS

TOMATO-BUTTER-LEEK SAUCE:

2 tablespoons dry white wine

2 tablespoons white wine vinegar

2 tablespoons minced shallots

1 bay leaf

Freshly ground pepper to taste

¼ cup heavy cream

2 leeks, white part only, sliced

¾ cup (1½ sticks) cold unsalted butter, cut into small pieces

4 small tomatoes, diced

3 tablespoons unsalted butter

1 pound sea scallops, patted dry with paper towels

1 cup seasoned bread crumbs (page 30)

1 tablespoon grated lemon zest

2 to 3 leeks, white part only, washed and julienned (about 2 cups)

TO MAKE THE SAUCE: In a small saucepan, combine the wine, vinegar, shallots, bay leaf, and pepper. Cook over medium heat for 8 to 10 minutes, or until reduced by half. Add the cream and leeks and cook for 3 to 5 minutes more, or until the leeks are nearly tender. Whisk in the butter, one piece at a time, and stir until smooth. Add the tomato and cook for 1 minute. Set aside and keep warm.

Preheat the broiler. In a large ovenproof skillet, melt 2 tablespoons of the butter over medium heat. Add the scallops and cook for 2 minutes on each side, or until opaque. Sprinkle with the bread crumbs and lemon zest,

and place under the broiler 4 inches from the heat source for 2 to 3 minutes, or until the crumbs are lightly browned.

Meanwhile, in a small saucepan, cook the julienned leeks in salted boiling water for 1 to 2 minutes, or until tender. Drain and add the remaining 1 tablespoon of butter.

To serve, divide the julienned leeks among 4 plates. Divide the scallops over the leeks and spoon the sauce over the top.

SERVES 4

Bryan Leech and Martin Marley have owned Kilgraney House, an 1820s country house retreat in Bagenalstown, County Carlow, since 1992. For many busy Dubliners, it's a weekend home away from home, chosen for its relaxed rural setting, its whimsical, artistic interior design, and the sumptuous, sophisticated meals prepared by Bryan and Martin, like this duck breast in a rich sweet-tart sauce. Serve it with Potato, Parsnip, and Apple Purée (page 111).

ROAST BREAST OF DUCK WITH DRIED SOUR CHERRY AND BALSAMIC SAUCE

6 boneless duck breast halves with skin (5 to 6 ounces each)

Sea salt and ground mixed peppercorns

1 tablespoon sunflower oil

SOUR CHERRY AND BALSAMIC SAUCE:

2½ cups homemade chicken stock or canned low-salt chicken broth

2 sage sprigs

2 tablespoons balsamic vinegar

2 tablespoons dried sour cherries

1 green onion, finely chopped

WILTED SPINACH:

2 tablespoons olive oil

1 clove shallot, minced

8 ounces baby spinach leaves, rinsed but not dried

Dash of ground nutmeg

Preheat the oven to 250°F. Trim the duck breasts and score the skin side. Season with salt and pepper. In a large ovenproof skillet, heat the oil over medium heat. Cook the duck breasts, skin-side up, for 2 minutes, then turn and cook for 5 minutes, or until still pink inside. Remove the skillet from the heat, turn the breasts over again, and place in the oven for up to 20 minutes while preparing the sauce.

TO MAKE THE SAUCE: In a small saucepan, cook the stock or broth and sage over medium heat for 10 to 15 minutes, or until reduced to about 1 cup. Add the vinegar and cook for 1 minute. Add the dried cherries and cook for 3 to 5 minutes, or until tender. Add the green onion and cook for 30 seconds.

TO MAKE THE WILTED SPINACH: In a large skillet, heat the olive oil over medium heat. Add the shallot and cook for about 1 minute, then add the spinach and stir constantly for 1 to 2 minutes, or until the greens are wilted. Season with a little nutmeg.

To serve, cut each duck breast into 10 to 12 slices. Place a little spinach in the center of each serving plate and top with duck slices. Spoon the sauce over the top.

SERVES 6

Boilie is a soft cheese made by Ann and John Brodie on their Ryefield Farm in County Cavan (see page 157). The word *boilie* (pronounced bowl-ee) comes from the old Irish word meaning "the place where cattle are led to be milked," and is made from both cow's and goat's milk. Patricia McInerney, chef-owner of Flapper's, in Tulla, County Clare, uses a combination of Boilie and cream cheese to stuff chicken breasts, which she serves with a piquant red pepper sauce. Accompany with Garlic Mashed Potatoes (page 101) and Mixed Beans with Bacon and Almonds (page 116).

BOILIE-STUFFED CHICKEN BREASTS WITH RED PEPPER CREAM SAUCE

RED PEPPER CREAM SAUCE:

2 red bell peppers, seeded and halved

½ cup dry white wine

2 tablespoons white vinegar

Pinch of a chicken bouillon cube

1 teaspoon sugar

1 cup heavy cream

8 balls Boilie goat cheese, or ¼ cup fresh white goat cheese at room temperature blended with 1 table-spoon olive oil

1 tablespoon cream cheese at room temperature

3 tablespoons minced fresh chervil, basil, or chives

1 tablespoon fresh lemon juice

Salt and freshly ground pepper to taste

4 bone-in chicken breast halves with skin (4 to 5 ounces each)

2 tablespoons melted unsalted butter mixed with 1 teaspoon minced garlic

2 tablespoons Boilie oil or canola oil

TO MAKE THE SAUCE: Preheat the broiler. Place the peppers in a baking pan skin-side up. Cook 6 inches from the heat source for 10 minutes on each side, or until the peppers are soft and the skin is loose. Remove from the oven and place in a closed paper bag to cool to the touch. Rub off the skin and cut the pepper into pieces.

In a small saucepan, combine the peppers, wine, and vinegar. Bring to a boil over medium heat, then reduce heat and simmer for 5 to 8 minutes, or until reduced by half. Add the pinch of bouillon cube, sugar, and cream and cook for 3 to 5 minutes, or until the sauce thickens. Transfer to a blender or food processor and process until smooth. Set aside.

In a small bowl, combine the Boilie or goat cheese, cream cheese, herbs, lemon juice, salt, and pepper. Stir to blend. With your fingers, gently loosen the skin from each chicken breast and spoon one-fourth of the stuffing under it. Press the skin down to seal and secure with a toothpick. Brush the skin with garlic butter.

Preheat the oven to 375°F. In a large skillet, heat the Boilie or canola oil over medium-high heat. Cook the chicken, skin-side down, for 2 to 3 minutes, or until lightly browned, then transfer to an ovenproof casserole dish. Bake for 35 to 40 minutes, or until the skin is crisp and the chicken is opaque throughout. Reheat the sauce.

To serve, place a chicken breast in the center of each serving plate and spoon the sauce over the top.

SERVES 4

In a former life, Lettercollum House, built in 1861 in Timoleague, County Cork, was a convent run by the Sisters of Mercy, so the house is complete with a chapel, stained-glass windows, and even a confessional. Today, the chapel serves as the restaurant of Con McLaughlin and Karen Austin's Victorian guest house. Much of the produce is grown in their walled organic garden, although Karen's cooking style reflects influences well beyond the boundaries of the property. This dish, typically featured on an autumn or winter menu, is made with pheasant, but Cornish hens, more widely available year-round, are a good substitute. Serve with Carrot and Turnip Purée (page 111).

CORNISH HENS WITH APRICOT, PORT, AND BALSAMIC SAUCE

2 Cornish hens, split down the center

Freshly ground pepper to taste

8 slices bacon

APRICOT, PORT, AND BALSAMIC SAUCE:

4 cups homemade chicken stock or canned low-salt chicken broth

½ cup port

1 cup dry red wine

⅔ cup (4 ounces) dried apricots, finely chopped

1 tablespoon balsamic vinegar

Salt and freshly ground pepper to taste

Preheat the oven to 400°F. Put the Cornish hen halves in an ovenproof baking pan, skin-side up. Sprinkle with pepper and cover with the bacon slices. Bake for 15 minutes, then reduce the oven temperature to 300°F and bake for 15 minutes, or until the skin is crisp. Remove from the oven and discard the bacon.

TO MAKE THE SAUCE: In a medium saucepan, bring the stock or broth to a boil over medium heat, then lower heat to a simmer and cook for 10 to 15 minutes, or until reduced to about 1 cup. In another saucepan, combine the port and red wine. Bring to a boil over medium heat, then lower heat to a simmer and cook for 8 to 10 minutes, or until reduced to about ½ cup.

Pour the reduced stock or broth into the reduced wine. Stir in the apricots and vinegar. Cook for 8 to 10 minutes, or until the sauce is reduced by one-third and is thickened. Season with salt and pepper.

To serve, place a Cornish hen half in the center of each serving plate and spoon the sauce over the top.

SERVES 4

Lettercollum House, Timoleague, County Cork.

Kinsale International Gourmet Festival

One of Ireland's most interesting food fests takes place in Kinsale, eighteen miles south of Cork City. In the heyday of sailing, Kinsale was the country's biggest port, with the most sheltered harbor. Today, it harbors more restaurants per square foot than any other town, and according to some researchers, more restaurants per capita than Paris. In the 1970s, the Kinsale Good Food Circle was formed by a group of restaurateurs who decided to work together to promote the town through a common bond of haute cuisine. The Circle launched the International Gourmet Festival in 1977, a weekend devoted to gourmet dining, eating, and drinking festivities, and like fine wine, it gets better with age.

The weekend is officially launched with a Champagne reception on Thursday night and concludes with a farewell brunch on Sunday. Sandwiched in between are cookery demonstrations, food exhibitions, a wine fair, cookbook signings, nightly dinners at Good Food Circle member restaurants, and a black-tie ball. A nightly Festival Club ensures conspicuous consumption! For details, see Resources (page 161).

Kinsale Restaurants

GOOD FOOD CIRCLE

A Actons Hotel
B Bernard's
C Bistro
D Blue Haven
E Cottage Loft
F Jim Edwards
H Man Friday
I Max's Wine Bar
J Seasons
L Trident Hotel
M Vintage
N White House

Kinsale, County Cork

Kinsale, County Cork

Kinsale, County Cork

Boneless pork tenderloin works well with a wide range of flavors, is simple to prepare, quick to cook, and because it's boneless, easy to present. Here, two respected Belfast gents—Nick Price, chef-owner of Nick's Warehouse, and Éamonn Ó Catháin, chef and radio and television broadcaster—dress it up with simple yet sophisticated sauces. Choose either apple-onion gravy from Chef Price, or the honey, whiskey, and green peppercorn sauce from Chef Ó Catháin.

LOIN OF PORK WITH TWO SAUCES

2 pork tenderloins (about 1 pound each)

Salt and freshly ground pepper to taste

1 tablespoon canola oil

APPLE-ONION GRAVY:

2 tablespoons unsalted butter

2 tablespoons canola oil

4 large onions, sliced

2 Bramley, Gala, or Braeburn apples, peeled, cored, and sliced

2 teaspoons minced fresh thyme

½ cup homemade chicken stock or canned low-salt chicken broth

4 cups unsweetened apple juice or Irish cider, preferably Magner's brand

Salt and freshly ground pepper to taste

Sugar to taste (optional)

HONEY, WHISKEY, AND GREEN PEPPERCORN SAUCE:

¾ cup dry white wine

2 cups homemade chicken stock or canned low-salt chicken broth

2 cups heavy cream

1 cup (2 sticks) cold unsalted butter, cut into small pieces

½ cup Irish whiskey, preferably Bushmills Black Bush

½ cup honey, preferably wild Irish honey

Salt and ground green peppercorns to taste

Preheat the oven to 350°F. Cut the tenderloins in half crosswise. Season with salt and pepper.

In a large ovenproof skillet, heat the oil over medium-high heat. Add the meat and sear for 2 minutes on each side. Transfer the meat to the oven and cook for 8 to 12 minutes, or until an instant-read thermometer inserted in a tenderloin registers 155°F. Using tongs, transfer the meat to a wire rack set over a platter.

TO MAKE THE APPLE-ONION GRAVY: In the same skillet, melt the butter with the oil over medium-low heat. Cook the onions for 3 to 5 minutes, or until lightly browned. Add the apples and thyme and cook for 4 to 5 minutes, or until the apples begin to soften. Add the stock or broth and apple juice or cider, and simmer, uncovered, for 20 minutes, or until slightly thickened. Add salt and pepper, and if necessary, a little sugar.

TO MAKE THE HONEY, WHISKEY, AND GREEN PEPPERCORN SAUCE: In the same skillet, cook the wine over medium heat for 4 to 5 minutes, or until reduced by half. Add the stock or broth and cook for 4 to 5 minutes, or until reduced by one-third. Add the cream and cook for 4 to 5 minutes, or until reduced again by one-third. Whisk in the butter, one piece at a time, and cook for 2 to 3 minutes, or until thickened. Stir in 2 tablespoons of the whiskey and 2 tablespoons of the honey, and cook for 3 to 5 minutes, or until smooth. Add the salt and pepper. If you wish, add the remaining whiskey, honey, and any meat juice.

Transfer the meat to a carving board and cut into thin slices. To serve, spoon a small amount of either sauce into the center of a serving plate and arrange the slices of meat around it.

SERVES 4

Paul and Maire Flynn's stylish restaurant is located in a beautifully restored stone building that was once a leather tannery in Dungarvan, County Waterford. Despite its well-worn exterior and the restaurant's use of traditional ingredients, what goes on inside the Tannery—from the contemporary design to the globally inspired cuisine—is absolutely up-to-the-minute. Paul serves this dish with Crubeen samosas (pig's trotters stuffed in Asian spring roll wrappers) on his regular menu, but Colcannon (page 98) is a simpler accompaniment.

ROAST BELLY OF PORK WITH CRISP BACON, BLACK PUDDING, AND APPLES

1 large onion, sliced

4 cloves garlic, chopped

4 to 5 sage leaves, minced

2 cups homemade chicken stock or canned low-salt chicken broth

1 pork belly, rind removed (about 5 pounds)

¼ cup cider

8 cloves

Pinch of ground allspice

Pinch of ground cinnamon

Salt and freshly ground pepper to taste

⅓ cup packed brown sugar

SAUCE:

2 cups beef stock or low-salt canned beef broth

Leaves from 4 to 5 sprigs sage, minced

1 tablespoon canola oil

4 slices bacon

4 slices black pudding, preferably Galtee brand

1 Granny Smith apple, peeled, cored, and sliced

Preheat the oven to 325°F. Place the onion in a single layer in a roasting pan. Sprinkle with the garlic and half the sage. Pour in the stock or broth. Place the pork on top and pour the cider over. Sprinkle with the remaining sage, the cloves, allspice, cinnamon, salt, and pepper. Cover with aluminum foil and cook, basting 2 to 3 times, for 3 hours, or until the pork is very tender.

Uncover and sprinkle the pork with the brown sugar. Increase the oven temperature to 400°F, return the pork to the oven, and cook for 20 minutes, or until the meat is glazed and golden brown. Transfer to a platter and keep warm.

TO MAKE THE SAUCE: In a small saucepan, combine the beef stock or broth and sage and bring to a boil over medium heat. Reduce the heat and simmer for 15 min-utes, or until reduced by half. Strain into a clean saucepan and keep warm.

In a large skillet, heat the oil over medium heat. Cook the bacon until crisp. Transfer to paper towels to drain. Cook the black pudding for 3 to 5 minutes on each side, or until crisp. Using a slotted metal spatula, transfer to paper towels to drain. Add the apple slices and cook for 2 to 3 minutes, or until soft. Transfer to a plate.

Transfer the meat to a carving board and cut into thin slices. Add any meat juices to the sauce. To serve, place slices of meat in the center of each serving plate with a slice of black pudding. Spoon the sauce over and crumble the bacon over. Garnish with the apple slices.

SERVES 4

Irish Stout: A History of the Black Stuff

The art of brewing is thought to have been born as many as six thousand years ago. Hieroglyphics have been found that seem to indicate brewing, and evidence of beer has been recorded in every culture. Next to water and wine, beer is the world's most universal drink.

The art of brewing spread across Europe to the fertile land of Ireland, where Neolithic inhabitants began an Irish brewing tradition by planting wheat and barley. By the fifth century, St. Patrick was reportedly traveling around Ireland with his own brewer, a priest called Mesan, and St. Brigid did the brewing for all the churches in the Kildare area.

In 1759, Arthur Guinness decided to try his luck at brewing and took a lease on a small, ill-equipped brewery at St. James's Gate in Dublin. He started brewing ale, but found that he had to compete with a new drink that had become popular with the porters at Covent Garden and Billingsgate in England. The new brew, affectionately nicknamed "porter," was a dark beer, made by adding roasted barley to the usual hops, yeast, and water. Determined to brew a better porter than his competitors, in 1822 Guinness laid down exact regulations for the brewing of his Extra Superior Porter. The word *stout*, meaning hearty and robust, was added in the early 1920s, and eventually the word evolved as a name in its own right.

Today, Guinness is Ireland's most popular brand, with Murphy's Irish Stout, brewed at Lady's Well Brewery in Cork City, second in the market. Both are widely available in the United States.

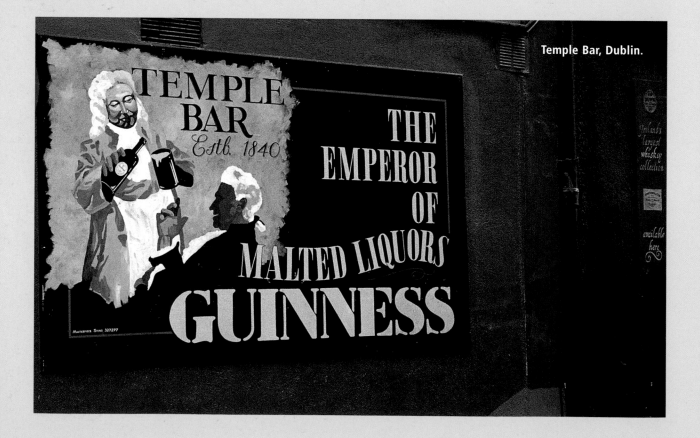

Temple Bar, Dublin.

Clonakilty, County Cork.

Dunbrody House in Arthurstown, County Wexford, is a member of the prestigious collection of Irish country homes listed in *The Blue Book*. Visiting one of them assures you of a comfortable stay in luxurious surroundings, as well as impeccable food and service in the dining room. Kevin and Catherine Dundon, hosts at Dunbrody, not only live up to such standards, they exceed them, as was proven by Dunbrody being named Country House of the Year by Irish food writer Georgina Campbell in her *2001 Guide to Ireland's Finest Places to Eat, Drink & Stay*. This updated recipe for a traditional loin of bacon was Kevin's entry into the annual Wedgwood Chef and Potter Competition. Serve it with Boxty (page 102) and Braised Cabbage (page 113).

LOIN OF BACON WITH CRANBERRY-CIDER JUS

1 loin of bacon or smoked pork shoulder (about 2 pounds)

8 cloves

½ onion, sliced

¼ cups honey

⅔ cup cider

½ cup fresh or thawed frozen cranberries

⅓ cup chicken stock or canned low-salt chicken broth

Salt and freshly ground pepper to taste

Place the bacon or smoked shoulder in a large saucepan and add cold water to cover. Bring to a boil over medium heat, then reduce heat to a simmer, cover, and cook for 30 to 35 minutes, or until nearly tender.

Preheat the oven to 325°F. Remove the meat from the pan, cut in half lengthwise if using bacon, and pierce each half with 4 cloves. Put the sliced onion in the bottom of an ovenproof roasting pan, place the meat on top, coat with honey, and roast for 20 minutes, or until the meat begins to brown and the onions start to caramelize.

Transfer the meat to a serving platter and keep warm. Add the cider to the baking pan and cook for 3 to 5 minutes, or until reduced by half. Add the cranberries and stock or broth and stir, scraping up the browned bits from the bottom of the pan, then cook until again reduced by half. Season with salt and pepper. Strain the sauce into a clean saucepan and keep warm.

Transfer the meat to a carving board and cut into thin slices. To serve, spoon some sauce into the center of each serving plate and fan slices of meat around the sauce.

SERVES 4

Celtic Cuisine

The traditional food and drink of the Celtic people was very much like what we call "health food" today. Dictated by circumstances and climate, it consisted mainly of root vegetables, grains, buttermilk, and a limited amount of meat and fish. It bred a race of people with the strength and stamina to spend long hours in the fields and to withstand the cold, damp climate of the Celtic nations of Ireland, Scotland, and Wales.

The Courtyard, Schull, County Cork.

Kay O'Dowd, Bunratty Folk Park, Bunratty, County Clare.

Butcher shop, Bandon, County Cork.

Some of the recipes in *The New Irish Table* are based on the legacy of Celtic cookery, both its ingredients and its traditional techniques. Galettes, crêpes, griddle cakes, and pancakes are all versions of flat breads that were cooked on a bake stone, griddle, or hearth iron.

Braised and stewed foods were another traditional fare of the Celtic nations, for burning fuels such as peat, coal, and charcoal made it necessary for most meals to be cooked in cauldrons and crocks over long periods of time. Irish stew is the best-known example.

The sweet-spicy blend of apricots and tarragon is perfect in this simple sauce for grilled or broiled lamb from chef Gerry Galvin, whom some call the father of modern Irish cooking. From Kinsale, County Cork, where he nudged the town into gourmet greatness, to Moycullen, County Galway, where he relocated to Drimcong House, Galvin's name and reputation are legendary. Serve this dish with Potato, Parsnip, and Apple Purée (page 111).

LAMB CUTLETS WITH HONEY, APRICOT, AND TARRAGON SAUCE

⅔ cup (4 ounces) dried apricots, finely chopped

2 cups chicken stock or canned low-salt chicken broth

2 tablespoons minced fresh tarragon

2½ tablespoons honey

2 teaspoons fresh lemon juice

Salt and freshly ground pepper to taste

1 teaspoon hot Thai curry paste

2 tablespoons olive oil

12 lamb cutlets or loin chops (2 pounds total)

Tarragon sprigs for garnish

Soak the apricots in the stock or broth with the minced tarragon for 3 to 4 hours.

Transfer the apricot mixture to a food processor. Add 1 teaspoon of the honey, the lemon juice, salt, and pepper, and process until smooth. Pour into a small saucepan and cook over medium heat for 1 to 2 minutes, or until heated through.

Light a fire in a charcoal grill or preheat a gas grill to medium-high. Combine the remaining honey, curry paste, and olive oil in a small bowl. Brush the mixture over both sides of the lamb cutlets. Season with salt and pepper. Grill the lamb for 3 minutes on each side for rare and 5 minutes on each side for medium.

To serve, arrange 3 cutlets on each serving plate and spoon the sauce over.

Garnish with tarragon sprigs.

SERVES 4

Chef Noel McMeel, a Toomebridge, County Antrim, native, honed his cooking skills with American chefs like Alice Waters and the late Jean-Louis Palladin before returning to Northern Ireland to open Trompets, his highly acclaimed restaurant in Magherafelt. Noel now serves as head chef at Castle Leslie, Glaslough, County Monaghan, where he adds eclectic touches to traditional recipes, like these lamb shanks, which he serves with Champ (page 101).

BRAISED LAMB SHANKS WITH ROASTED GARDEN VEGETABLES

3 tablespoons olive oil

4 lamb shanks (¾ to 1 pound each)

1 large carrot, diced

1 onion, diced

1 stalk celery, diced

½ cup dry white wine

14 ounces canned diced tomatoes

4 to 5 sprigs thyme

1 bay leaf

2 cloves garlic, minced

1 cup water

Salt and freshly ground pepper to taste

ROASTED GARDEN VEGETABLES:

1 small turnip, cut into 1-inch pieces

1 carrot, cut into 1-inch pieces

1 parsnip, cut into 1-inch pieces

1 onion, quartered

2 tablespoons olive oil

Salt and freshly ground pepper to taste

In a large skillet, heat the olive oil over medium heat. Cook the lamb on all sides until browned, about 5 minutes. Transfer to a Dutch oven or ovenproof casserole dish. Add the diced vegetables to the skillet and cook for 5 minutes over medium heat, or until soft. Add the white wine and stir, scraping up the browned bits from the bottom of the pan, and cook for 3 to 5 minutes, or until the wine is reduced by half. Transfer the vegetables and cooking liquid to the Dutch oven or casserole.

Add the tomatoes, thyme, bay leaf, garlic, water, salt, and pepper to the Dutch oven or casserole, cover, and simmer for 2 hours, or until the lamb is fork tender.

Preheat the oven to 400°F. Place the turnip, carrot, parsnip, and onion in a single layer in the bottom of a roasting pan. Toss with the olive oil and sprinkle with salt and pepper. Cook for 20 to 25 minutes, stirring once or twice, or until the vegetables are soft and lightly browned.

Using a slotted metal spatula, transfer the lamb shanks to a platter, cover, and keep warm. Strain the sauce through a fine sieve into a clean saucepan, pressing the vegetables through with the back of a large spoon. Cook over low heat for 5 minutes, until the sauce is thickened. Set aside and keep warm.

To serve, place a lamb shank in the center of each serving plate, spoon the sauce over, and surround with the roasted vegetables.

SERVES 4

Wild game in season has always been an important part of the Irish diet, but farm-raised game, especially venison, is now a year-round affair at Crookedwood House, which originally served as Taghmon Parish rectory across from Lough Derravaragh, Mullingar, County Westmeath. Chef-owner Noel Kenny's skilled use of local produce, meat, and game—as in this French-style stew—has earned Crookedwood House a place as the premier dining-out venue in the midlands. Try this dish with Colcannon (page 98), or Mashed Potatoes with Turnip and Buttermilk (page 98).

BURGUNDY VENISON

3 tablespoons sunflower oil

8 slices bacon

2 onions, diced

2 pounds venison, cut into 2-inch chunks

2 tablespoons flour

2 cups dry red wine

2 cups beef stock or canned low-salt beef broth

3 cloves garlic, crushed

Grated zest of 1 orange

6 juniper berries, crushed

Bouquet garni: 2 sprigs *each* parsley, thyme, and tarragon tied in a cheesecloth square

Salt and freshly ground pepper to taste

12 large white mushrooms

2 tablespoons minced fresh flat-leaf parsley

In a Dutch oven or heavy ovenproof casserole, heat the oil over medium heat. Add the bacon and cook for 5 minutes on each side, or until crisp. Using tongs, transfer to paper towels to drain. Add the onions to the pan and sauté for 3 to 5 minutes, or until browned. Add the venison and cook for 2 to 3 minutes, turning once or twice. Sprinkle the meat and onions with the flour, stir until coated, and cook for about 2 minutes. Stir in the wine, stock or broth, garlic, orange zest, and juniper berries. Bring to a boil, then reduce heat to a simmer. Add the bouquet garni, salt, and pepper.

Cover and cook for 1½ hours, or until the meat is tender and the sauce is thick. If the sauce becomes too thick, add extra stock or broth, or water. Add the bacon and mushrooms, and cook, uncovered, for 20 minutes. Discard the bouquet garni. Taste and adjust the seasoning.

To serve, spoon the stew into the center of each serving plate and sprinkle with the parsley.

SERVES 4

For many years, beef was not an integral part of the Irish diet, as farmers kept cows more for their milk than for their meat. Today, however, beef is popular, and beyond the traditional Sunday roast you'll find many beef dishes prepared using what would have once been considered unusual ingredients. This recipe, from the late chef Bill Patterson, proprietor of the Oystercatcher, Oysterhaven, County Cork, is from *The Cork Cook Book,* a wonderful selection of recipes that highlight the culinary genius of Cork chefs. The book was a fund-raising project of the Cork Simon Community, which provides services to homeless people and campaigns for justice. Serve this dish with Garlic Mashed Potatoes (page 101) or Mashed Potatoes with Turnip and Buttermilk (page 98).

MEDALLIONS OF BEEF WITH PORT SAUCE AND CASHEL BLUE CHEESE

¼ cup golden raisins

1 cup port

4 beef filet steaks (about 6 ounces each)

2 tablespoons olive oil

2 shallots, finely minced

Salt and freshly ground pepper to taste

3 tablespoons water

2 tablespoons pine nuts

½ cup (1 stick) cold unsalted butter, cut into small pieces

1 tablespoon Dijon mustard

1 tablespoon fresh lemon juice

8 ounces Cashel Blue cheese or other blue cheese, crumbled

Minced fresh chives for garnish

One day before serving, soak the raisins in the port for 10 to 12 hours. Strain and reserve the raisins and the port.

Coat the beef with the olive oil. In a large skillet over medium-high heat, cook the steaks for 4 to 5 minutes on each side for medium-rare. Remove to an ovenproof dish, sprinkle with the shallots, and season with salt and pepper. Cover and keep warm.

Add the water to the same pan and bring it to a boil over medium heat. Stir, scraping up the browned bits from the bottom of the pan, and cook for 2 to 3 minutes, or until reduced by two-thirds. Stir in the reserved raisins and port, then add the pine nuts. Reduce the heat to low and whisk in the pieces of butter, a few at a time, cook for 3 to 5 minutes, or until the sauce thickens. Add the mustard and any juices that have collected from the steaks. Season with salt and pepper and the lemon juice.

To serve, preheat the broiler. Cover each steak with the crumbled blue cheese, place under the broiler 4 inches from the heat source for 1 to 2 minutes, or until the cheese is lightly browned and bubbling. Transfer each steak to a serving plate and spoon the sauce around the meat. Garnish with the chives.

SERVES 4

Great Markets

The tradition of market shopping is finally seeing a revival in Ireland. For centuries, farmers and food producers brought their produce to city markets to sell butter, milk, meat, and fish, and in rural areas, entire towns sprung up around market squares where the buying and selling of cattle, sheep, pigs, and produce took place.

Thanks to increased awareness of the benefits of organic produce, and the desire for fewer mass-produced products, market shopping for artisanal foods—from home-made bread and farmhouse cheese to olive oil and sausages—is popular again.

The English Market, off the Grand Parade in Cork City, is one of the country's biggest and best, a unique blend of old traders selling fish and meat from stalls their families have held for generations—Tim O'Sullivan and Son, Liam Bresnan's, Ashley O'Neill, and Kay O'Connell, to name a few—with new dealers like the Alternative Bread Company and Mr. Bell's Oriental Food dispensing everthing from pasta and pesto to hand-cured olives and exotic spices.

Farmhouse cheeses are gaining in popularity throughout Ireland, and beyond the English Market you'll find a wide variety at Val Manning's Emporium in Ballylickey, near Bantry, County Cork. Manning has been a great ambassador for the high-quality regional produce he stocks in his shop, which is beloved by chefs and food-lovers. His hospitality is legendary, and is never more obvious than when he's hosting one of his West Cork Food and Drink Fairs. His once-annual house party has been going strong since the late 1970s, when he took over the shop from his parents and invited nearby cheese makers and salmon smokers to showcase their wares. The Fair has gained so much interest and attention that the area can handle the crowds only on alternating years now instead of yearly. Otherwise, Mannings is open for business daily, selling the finest cheeses, wines, breads, cold meats, and

Sheridans Cheesemongers, Churchyard Street, Galway.

Temple Bar Market, Dublin.

smoked salmon, which you're free to enjoy picnic-style at one of the whiskey-barrel tables in the front of the shop.

In both Galway (Churchyard Street) and Dublin (South Anne Street), brothers Seamus and Kevin Sheridan offer one of the largest selections of regional and European farm cheeses at their Sheridans Cheesemongers shops. They first began at the Galway Saturday market, where they gathered some of Ireland's beautiful farm cheeses to sell at their small stall. Encouraged by the enthusiasm of their customers, they set up their first shop in Galway. They later established the Temple Bar Saturday Market in Dublin with other specialty foods producers and traders, and later opened a shop there as well. Both are packed from floor to ceiling with Cheddars from Somerset, farm Goudas from Cork and Holland, rows of Stiltons and Irish blues, washed-rind cheeses from West Cork, and fresh goat cheeses from both County Clare and France, along with salami and pots of olives from Italy, Connemara honey, homemade jams, and organic pastas.

Mannings Emporium, Ballylickey, County Cork.

When locals give directions to the sumptuous Park Hotel in Kenmare, County Kerry, they need only say, "It's at the top of the town." True in both location and service, the hotel has been under the direction of Francis Brennan since 1985. Several well-known Irish chefs have been tutored under Brennan's direction, and each has lived up to or exceeded expectations at this beautiful hotel, built in 1897 by the Great Southern and Western Railway Company. Head chef Joe Ryan is no exception. He showcases Kerry lamb and Kerry seafood, but also features seasonal specialties, like this rabbit dish, an autumn favorite, which he serves with a rich wild-mushroom broth. Accompany it with Murphy's in a Clogher Valley Mist (page 106).

SEARED LOIN OF RABBIT WITH VEGETABLE RAGOUT AND WILD MUSHROOM BROTH

2 cups sunflower oil

2 tablespoons minced mixed fresh herbs

2 garlic gloves

1 loin of rabbit (about 2½ pounds)

WILD MUSHROOM BROTH:

2 tablespoons unsalted butter

2 tablespoons sunflower oil

¼ cup chopped onion

5 cloves garlic, minced

1 pound mixed wild mushrooms, chopped

½ cup Madeira

4 cups chicken stock or canned low-salt chicken broth

Salt and freshly ground pepper to taste

VEGETABLE RAGOUT:

1 bunch baby carrots, trimmed

2 leeks, white part only, sliced

1 pound green beans, trimmed

1 pound asparagus, trimmed

8 ounces mixed wild mushrooms, chopped

Salt and freshly ground pepper to taste

1 tablespoon unsalted butter

Chervil sprigs for garnish

In a large self-sealing plastic bag, combine the oil, herbs, and garlic. Remove and reserve 3 tablespoons to sauté the rabbit later. Add the rabbit to the bag, seal, and refrigerate overnight. Remove from the refrigerator and drain.

TO MAKE THE BROTH: In a large skillet, melt the butter with the oil over medium heat. Add the onion and garlic and sauté for 5 to 8 minutes, or until browned. Add the mushrooms and sauté for 3 to 5 minutes, or until soft. Add the Madeira and cook for 8 to 10 minutes, or until reduced by half. Add the stock or broth, salt, and pepper. Reduce heat and simmer for 35 to 40 minutes, or until the liquid is reduced to about 1½ cups. Remove from heat and let cool. Strain, return to the pan, and simmer for 10 to 15 minutes to concentrate the flavor. Remove from heat and keep warm.

TO MAKE THE RAGOUT: In a large skillet, bring 2 cups salted water to a boil over medium heat. Add the carrots, leeks, green beans, and asparagus, cover, and cook for 8 to 10 minutes, or until crisp-tender. Drain and add the mushrooms, salt, pepper, and butter. Remove from heat and keep warm.

In a large skillet, heat the reserved 3 tablespoons herb oil over medium heat. Add the rabbit, season with salt and pepper, and sauté for 3 to 5 minutes on each side, or until lightly browned. Keep warm.

To serve, spoon the vegetable ragout into shallow soup bowls. Cut the rabbit into 4 pieces and arrange 1 piece on top each serving of vegetables. Spoon the mushroom broth over the top. Garnish with chervil sprigs.

SERVES 4

Timolin Pewter Mill, Timolin, County Kildare.

Chef Cath Gradwell, who worked with Rowley Leigh in London's Kensington Place, and with Paul Rankin in Roscoff, Belfast, was named one of Ten Chefs to Watch Out For by noted Irish food writer John McKenna. Gradwell, now cooking at Alden's in Belfast, was described by McKenna as "demonstrating a commanding technique . . . with a true concern for every detail of every dish." This bold-flavored dish is a perfect example of Gradwell's skill. Serve with Champ (page 101).

BLACK PUDDING–STUFFED BREAST OF PHEASANT WITH MUSTARD CREAM SAUCE

6 tablespoons canola oil

4 slices black pudding, preferably Galtee brand

4 boneless, skinless pheasant breast halves (about 6 ounces each)

Salt and freshly ground pepper to taste

⅔ cup all-purpose flour

4 eggs, beaten

1½ cups seasoned bread crumbs (page 30)

2 tablespoons unsalted butter

MUSTARD CREAM SAUCE:

2 cups heavy cream

2 tablespoons whole-grain mustard, preferably Lakeshore brand

2 chicken bouillon cubes

2 teaspoons fresh lemon juice

Salt and freshly ground pepper to taste

Preheat the oven to 400°F. In a large ovenproof skillet, heat 2 tablespoons of the oil over medium heat. Add the black pudding and cook for 3 to 5 minutes on each side, or until crisp. Using a slotted metal spatula, transfer to paper towels to drain.

With a sharp knife, cut a horizontal pocket in the thick side of each pheasant breast. Season inside and out with salt and pepper. Cut each black pudding slice in half and place 2 halves side-by-side in each pocket. Press the skin down to close the pocket. Dredge the breasts in the flour, then in the eggs and bread crumbs. Refrigerate for 10 minutes.

In the same skillet, melt the butter with the remaining 4 tablespoons oil over medium heat. Add the pheasant breasts and brown quickly on each side. Transfer to the preheated oven and roast, turning once or twice, for 10 to 12 minutes, or until golden brown. Remove and keep warm.

MUSTARD CREAM SAUCE: In a small saucepan, heat the cream over medium heat to a simmer. Reduce heat to low and stir in the mustard, bouillon cubes, lemon juice, salt, and pepper. Stir until the bouillon cubes have dissolved. Remove from the heat and keep warm.

To serve, place 1 pheasant breast on each serving plate and spoon the sauce over.

SERVES 4

Tuesday Lunch.

Soupe au Pistou.   3.50 / 5.50

Pepper Pot Soup   3.75 / 5.75.

Mussel + Smoked Fish Chowder 3.75 / 5.75.

Crab Cakes w/ Piquant Mayo 4.75 / 6.75.

Cherry Tomato + Goat's Cheese Pizza. 6.95.

Emmental + Asparagus Tart   5.75.

Chicken Confit w/ Wild Rice + Puy Lentil Risotto 7.95

Roast Smoked Ham w/ Sage + Mustard Mash   8.75.

Spiced Lamb Patties w/ Chargrilled
                                                      Ratatouille 8.75.

Chargrilled Tuna Steak Club Sandwich 10.95.

Pecan Pie
Lemon Tart
                                          } 4.25.
Irish Strawberries + Cream
Tart Tatin

SIDE DISHES

Opposite, top: Quin Abbey, Quin, County Clare. Opposite, bottom: Original Croom Mills, Croom, County Limerick.

Colcannon (from the Irish *cal ceann fhionn,* or "white-headed cabbage") is a mashed potato dish flavored with kale or cabbage. It's the traditional dish of the Halloween (All Hallow's Eve) dinner, but is served year-round by home cooks and restaurant chefs alike.

COLCANNON

1 pound cabbage, cored, quartered, and shredded

2 pounds boiling potatoes, peeled and cut into 2-inch pieces

2 small leeks, including white and green parts, washed and sliced

1 cup milk

Salt and freshly ground pepper to taste

½ teaspoon ground mace

8 tablespoons (1 stick) unsalted butter, plus 2 tablespoons butter, cut into small pieces

In separate saucepans, cook the cabbage and potatoes in salted boiling water for 12 to 15 minutes, or until tender. Drain the cabbage and chop. Drain the potatoes and mash.

Meanwhile, in a large saucepan, combine the leeks and milk. Bring to a simmer and cook for 8 to 10 minutes, or until the leeks are tender. Add the potatoes, salt, pepper, and mace to the pan and stir over low heat until well blended. Add the cabbage and 8 tablespoons butter and stir again until blended. Dot with the 2 tablespoons butter. Serve at once.

SERVES 4 TO 6

MASHED POTATOES WITH TURNIP AND BUTTERMILK: Substitute 1 pound turnips, peeled and cut into 1-inch pieces, for the cabbage, and 1 cup buttermilk for the milk. Combine the mashed potatoes and mashed turnips, stir in the buttermilk, and season with salt and pepper. Sprinkle with minced fresh chives.

Champ, which is sometimes called "poundies," is a mixture of potatoes and green onions served in a mound with a well of melted butter in the center. Traditionally, it's eaten with a spoon, starting from the outside of the mound and dipping each spoonful into the butter.

CHAMP

2 pounds boiling potatoes, peeled and cut into 2-inch pieces

½ cup half-and-half

6 tablespoons unsalted butter

1⅓ cups minced fresh chives or green onions (including green parts)

Salt and freshly ground pepper to taste

Cook the potatoes in salted boiling water 12 to 15 minutes, or until tender. Drain and mash.

Meanwhile, in a medium saucepan over low heat, combine the half-and-half and 4 tablespoons of the butter. Heat until the butter is melted. Add the chives or green onions, reduce heat to a simmer, and cook for 2 to 4 minutes, or until the chives or green onions are soft.

Add the potatoes, salt, and pepper to the milk mixture and stir until blended. To serve, spoon the champ into a deep bowl, make a well in the center, and top with the remaining 2 tablespoons butter.

SERVES 4

GARLIC MASHED POTATOES: Substitute 1 cup finely chopped onions and 3 tablespoons finely minced garlic, sautéed in ½ cup (1 stick) unsalted butter for the chives or green onions. Add the onion mixture to the mashed potatoes, stir in the half-and-half, and season with salt and pepper.

The word **boxty** is derived from the Irish *bac-staí,* referring to the traditional cooking of potatoes on the hob *(bac)* over an open fire *(staí).* Generally, boxty is a mix of grated raw and cooked mashed potatoes, patted together in the shape of a small cake and fried. Variations, however, are numerous. This one from chef Máighréad Forde of Bricín, a restaurant and craft shop in Killarney, County Kerry, is made from grated potatoes only and includes onions. Forde serves her boxty with dishes like bacon and cabbage or Irish stew.

BOXTY

1 pound boiling potatoes, peeled

1 large onion, finely chopped

2 eggs, beaten

½ teaspoon salt

½ teaspoon freshly ground pepper

Pinch of ground nutmeg

2 tablespoons flour

2 to 4 tablespoons unsalted butter for frying

Line a large bowl with a piece of muslin or cheesecloth, or a clean linen towel. Using the large holes of a box grater, grate the potatoes into the bowl. Squeeze the cloth to extract as much of the starchy liquid as possible. Discard the starchy liquid, return the potatoes to the bowl, and stir in the onion, eggs, salt, pepper, and nutmeg. Add the flour and mix well.

In a large skillet, melt 2 tablespoons of the butter over medium heat. Drop the potato mixture, 1 tablespoonful at a time, into the skillet; do not crowd the pan. Flatten each cake with a spatula and cook for 3 to 4 minutes on each side, or until lightly browned and crisp. Transfer the cakes to a baking sheet and keep warm in a 200°F oven. Repeat until all the mixture is used, adding more butter as necessary. Serve immediately.

MAKES ABOUT 16 POTATO CAKES

VARIATION: Cut half the potatoes into 2-inch pieces. Cook the cut-up potatoes in salted boiling water for 12 to 15 minutes, or until tender. Drain and mash. Grate the other half, then combine the mashed potatoes with the grated potatoes. Substitute ½ cup of buttermilk for the beaten eggs. Proceed as above.

PARSNIP-POTATO CAKES: Peel 1½ pounds baking potatoes and 1½ pounds parsnips. Cut into 2-inch pieces. Cook separately in salted boiling water for 15 minutes, or until tender. Drain and mash the potatoes. Drain and mash the parsnips, then transfer to a food processor or blender and process for 1 to 2 minutes, or until smooth. Add the puréed parsnips, 2 beaten eggs, ½ cup half-and-half, 4 tablespoons unsalted butter, and ⅓ cup flour to the mashed potatoes. Season with salt and pepper to taste, form into cakes, and cook as above.

Sir Walter Raleigh and The Potato

There's some debate on how the potato, Ireland's best-known food, was brought there. Some historians claim that Sir Walter Raleigh planted the first potato in Europe in 1585 in a garden at Myrtle Grove, his gabled Elizabethan mansion in Youghal (pronounced *yawl*), County Cork. Raleigh was granted Irish lands by Elizabeth I for his help in putting down the Desmond Rebellion of 1579, and served as the mayor, or warden, of Youghal in 1588. Others claim that Raleigh first showed his New World discovery to Queen Elizabeth, who exclaimed: "It's a tuber, it's ugly, give it to the Irish!"

Another story says the potato was introduced to Europe as a result of Sir Francis Drake's voyage to South America, where the potato had been cultivated by the Incas for centuries, while others believe the potato was swept ashore from the wrecks of the Spanish Armada along the coast of Ireland.

Dublin Market.

Dublin Market.

Whichever story, if any, is true, the potato has been a mainstay of Irish cuisine for centuries. For generations, the Irish were totally dependent on this vegetable, which proved to be a remarkably healthy and economical foodstuff when supplemented by oatmeal and dairy products. By the early 1600s, the potato was Ireland's major crop and it continued as such until September 1845, when the potato blight appeared in Counties Waterford and Wexford. By the next summer, the blight had swept Ireland and the Great Hunger had begun.

One of Ireland's most inspired chefs, Denis Cotter is chef-owner of Café Paradiso in Cork, widely accepted as the best vegetarian restaurant in Ireland. Cotter has established an international reputation for innovation and uses the finest seasonal organic produce to create dishes bursting with flavor and richness. These crisp potato cakes, which he might serve with a flageolet bean dish or a vegetable stew at his restaurant, are laced with a healthy dose of mature Cashel Blue cheese and fresh herbs.

BLUE CHEESE POTATO CAKES

1½ to 1¾ pounds baking potatoes, peeled and cut into 2-inch pieces

2 tablespoons unsalted butter

2 tablespoons minced fresh chives

1 tablespoon minced garlic

¼ teaspoon ground nutmeg

Salt and freshly ground pepper to taste

2 tablespoons minced fresh dill

2 tablespoons minced fresh flat-leaf parsley

1 cup (4 ounces) Cashel Blue cheese or other blue cheese, crumbled

1 egg yolk

1 cup all-purpose flour

2 eggs beaten with ½ cup milk

1 to 1½ cups seasoned bread crumbs (page 30)

1 to 1½ cups canola oil

Sour cream or crème fraîche (recipe follows) for topping

Cook the potatoes in salted boiling water for 12 to 15 minutes, or until tender. Drain and mash. In a small skillet, melt the butter over low heat. Cook the chives and garlic for 1 to 2 minutes, or until soft. Stir into the mashed potatoes. Stir in the nutmeg, salt, pepper, dill, and parsley. Remove from heat and cool completely. Stir in the cheese and egg yolk. The cheese should remain in lumps scattered through the potatoes.

Shape the potato mixture into 12 cakes and refrigerate for 10 minutes to firm. Lightly dredge in flour and coat with the egg mixture, then the bread crumbs. In a large skillet, heat the oil over medium-high heat. Add the cakes and cook for 3 to 5 minutes on each side, or

until browned. (The cakes can be prepared ahead up to this point.)

To serve, place on a baking sheet and reheat in a 250°F oven for about 5 minutes. Serve with a dollop of sour cream or crème fraîche on top.

MAKES 12 SERVINGS

Crème Fraîche

Combine 1 cup heavy cream and 2 tablespoons buttermilk in a glass container, cover, and let stand at room temperature overnight, or until it becomes very thick. Stir well before refrigerating for up to 10 days.

Grange Lodge, a small Georgian country house in Dungannon, County Tyrone, is renowned for Norah Brown's hospitality and her cooking. Whatever is local—whether it's seasonal produce; whiskey from Bushmills, Northern Ireland's oldest distillery; or cheese from the nearby Fivemiletown Creamery—finds a place on the Grange Lodge table. Brown named this gratin-like potato dish in honor of the charming Clogher Valley, where Dungannon is situated.

MURPHY'S IN A CLOGHER VALLEY MIST

1½ pounds boiling potatoes, unpeeled

2 tablespoons unsalted butter

4 slices bacon

½ cup heavy cream

1 cup (4 ounces) shredded
  Fivemiletown Smoked Cheddar or
  other smoked Cheddar cheese

Salt and freshly ground pepper to taste

Preheat the oven to 400°F. Butter a baking pan.

Cook the potatoes in salted boiling water for 15 to 18 minutes, or until tender. Drain and let cool to the touch. Cut each potato into 4 wedges. Place the wedges, skin-side down, in the prepared pan and toss with the butter.

In a large skillet over medium heat, cook the bacon until crisp. Using a slotted metal spatula, transfer to paper towels to drain.

Pour the cream over the potatoes, sprinkle with the grated cheese and crumble the bacon over. Season with salt and pepper and bake for 20 to 25 minutes, or until the cream has thickened and the cheese has melted.

SERVES 4

Near Croagh Patrick, Murrisk, County Mayo.

These are baked potatoes with a little panache. I've also seen them called "fanned," or "hasselback," because of their distinctive shape, but regardless of the name, they couldn't be easier to make or prettier to look at. Delicious with poultry, meat, or game.

ACCORDION POTATOES

6 baking potatoes (about 2 pounds total), scrubbed

Olive oil for drizzling

Sea salt for sprinkling

1 bunch rosemary

Shredded Cheddar cheese for sprinkling (optional)

Preheat the oven to 400°F. Put each potato on a cutting board and lay a wooden spoon next to it. Cut each potato into 8 to 10 slices three-quarters of the way through, bringing the knife down until you reach the handle of the spoon. This will leave the base of the potato intact.

Put the potatoes in a roasting pan, drizzle with olive oil, and sprinkle with salt. Place a sprig of rosemary between each slice. Bake for 40 to 50 minutes, or until tender. Remove the rosemary sprigs and replace with fresh ones for serving, or sprinkle the potatoes with cheese, if you wish.

SERVES 6

Spuds and More

Although potatoes are the food most frequently associated with Ireland, other vegetables such as leeks, carrots, watercress, nettles, and garlic predate them. Cabbage, parsnips, onion, and turnips, which were easy to grow in Ireland's cool climate and have excellent keeping qualities, have also always been popular.

These traditional vegetables continue to star on the Irish table in interesting new combinations. Mashed potatoes—white, yellow, or red—are the basis for a wide range of traditional dishes, colcannon and champ especially, and they also appear mixed with turnips and flavored with buttermilk or smashed with garlic and topped with bacon. The traditional potato cake known as boxty may begin with grated and mashed potatoes, but other cakes and mashes combine parsnips, carrots, turnips, mushrooms, and even crumbled blue cheese. And creamy purées and gratins, rich with butter and cheese, are pure indulgences alongside poultry, meat, and game.

Swords, County Dublin.

POTATOES NEW SEASONS RUSH QUEENS

Vegetable purées are suddenly fashionable Irish fare despite the fact that the ingredients are quite traditional. Parsnips, for example, which taste sweeter after the first frost when their starch is converted to sugar, and both turnips and rutabagas (known in Ireland as Swedes), which are easy to grow and can be stored for long periods of time, have always been popular in Ireland and northern Europe and are delicious baked, boiled, or mashed. "It's all in the mix . . . in the way they're combined," a Cork chef confided, "and the smoother the better."

POTATO, PARSNIP, AND APPLE PURÉE WITH PARSNIP CRISPS

2 pounds parsnips, peeled and cut into 1-inch pieces

2 pounds baking potatoes, peeled and cut into 1-inch pieces

½ cup water

1½ pounds Granny Smith apples, peeled, cored, and sliced

2 cups milk

½ cup plus 2 tablespoons (1¼ sticks) unsalted butter, cut into pieces

Salt and freshly ground pepper to taste

Parsnip Crisps (page 37)

Cook the parsnips and potatoes in a large saucepan of salted boiling water for 20 to 25 minutes, or until tender. Drain and mash. Return to the saucepan.

In a medium saucepan, bring the water to a simmer over low heat. Add the apples, cover, and cook for 20 to 25 minutes, or until soft. Drain and mash.

Combine the mashed apples with the mashed potatoes and parsnips. In a medium saucepan, bring the milk to a boil over medium heat. With a hand-held electric mixer or immersion blender, add the milk and butter to the vegetable mixture and blend until smooth. Stir over medium heat until heated through. Season with salt and pepper and sprinkle with the Parsnip Crisps.

SERVES 8

PARSNIP AND TURNIP PURÉE: Peel 3 pounds parsnips and 1 pound turnips, and cut them into 1-inch pieces. Cook in salted boiling water for 30 to 40 minutes, or until tender. Drain and mash. Transfer to a food processor, add ½ cup (1 stick) unsalted butter at room temperature, ½ teaspoon ground nutmeg, and ½ cup minced fresh flat-leaf parsley, and process until smooth. Season with salt and pepper to taste and sprinkle with the parsnip crisps.

CARROT AND TURNIP PURÉE: Peel 2 pounds carrots and 2 pounds turnips, and cut them into 1-inch pieces. Cook in salted boiling water for 30 to 40 minutes, or until tender. Drain and mash. Transfer to a food processor. Add ½ cup sour cream, ¼ teaspoon ground ginger, and 4 tablespoons unsalted butter at room temperature, and process until smooth. Season with salt and pepper. Sprinkle with minced fresh chives.

CARROT PURÉE WITH GINGER AND ORANGE: Peel 4 pounds carrots and cut into ½-inch pieces. Cook with 3 tablespoons sugar in salted boiling water for 20 to 25 minutes, or until tender. Drain and mash. Transfer to a food processor. Add ⅓ cup orange juice, ½ cup (1 stick) unsalted butter at room temperature, 1½ tablespoons minced fresh ginger, 1 tablespoon grated orange zest, 1 tablespoon fresh lemon juice, and 1 tablespoon sugar. Process until smooth. Season with salt and pepper to taste.

If you don't already keep frozen peas on hand, this recipe will give you reason to start. Devised by chef Colin O'Daly of the renowned Roly's Bistro in Ballsbridge, Dublin (and since 1998 in North Palm Beach, Florida), the purée is delicious with grilled fish like salmon or scallops, and it's flavorful enough to pair with heartier meats like roast beef or lamb.

MINTED PEA PURÉE

One 10-ounce package frozen peas

2 tablespoons unsalted butter

¼ cup finely chopped onion

1 clove garlic, minced

½ cup dry white wine

½ cup half-and-half

1 tablespoon minced fresh mint

Salt and freshly ground pepper to taste

In a small saucepan, cook the peas in a small amount of salted boiling water for 6 to 8 minutes, or until almost tender. Drain and set aside.

In a small skillet, melt the butter over medium heat. Add the onion and garlic and sauté for 3 to 5 minutes, or until tender. Add the white wine and cook until most of the wine has evaporated. Add the peas and half-and-half. Cook over medium-high heat for 2 to 3 minutes, or until the peas are tender. Drain, reserving the liquid.

Transfer the peas to a food processor and pulse for 10 to 15 seconds, or until nearly smooth. Add some of the reserved liquid, if necessary, to thin. Add the mint and pulse 2 to 3 times to incorporate. Return the purée to the skillet to heat, if necessary. Season with salt and pepper and serve hot.

SERVES 6

If the thought of cabbage reminds you of the days when most vegetables in Ireland were boiled to a pulp, try this slightly wilted, nearly caramelized version that includes tangy horseradish, garlic, and shallots. It's a perfect sidekick to pork.

BRAISED CABBAGE

2 tablespoons sunflower oil

4 shallots, finely diced

1 head savoy or napa cabbage, shredded

1 teaspoon prepared horseradish

1 clove garlic, minced

1 tablespoon grated fresh ginger

1 tablespoon sugar

2½ tablespoons white wine vinegar

1 tablespoon fresh lemon juice

Salt and freshly ground pepper to taste

In a heavy saucepan, heat the sunflower oil over medium-high heat. Add the shallots, cabbage, horseradish, garlic, and ginger and sauté for 5 to 8 minutes, or until the cabbage starts to wilt. Stir in the sugar and cook to carmelize the cabbage lightly. Add the vinegar and lemon juice and stir to scrape up the browned bits from the bottom of the pan. Season with salt and pepper. Serve immediately.

SERVES 6

Pommes Anna, or "Anna potatoes," is a classic French dish of baked, thinly sliced potatoes. A contemporary Irish version uses turnips instead of potatoes and adds bacon and Dubliner cheese for a distinctive touch. James Joyce fans will recognize the name Anna Livia from the writer's reference to the River Liffey, which he called Anna Livia Plurabell in his *Finnegans Wake*.

TURNIPS ANNA LIVIA

6 tablespoons unsalted butter, melted

½ cup all-purpose flour

½ cup (2 ounces) grated Dubliner or white Cheddar cheese

Salt and freshly ground pepper to taste

¼ teaspoon minced fresh thyme, plus more for garnish

¼ teaspoon minced fresh rosemary

Pinch of ground nutmeg

1¾ to 2 pounds white turnips, peeled and thinly sliced

6 slices bacon, cooked and crumbled

¼ cup heavy cream

Preheat the oven to 450°F. Brush the bottom and sides of a 9-inch pie plate with some of the melted butter.

In a small bowl, combine the flour, cheese, salt, pepper, the ¼ teaspoon thyme, the rosemary, and nutmeg. Arrange a single layer of the largest turnip slices in a concentric circle in the bottom and up the sides of the plate. Sprinkle some of the flour mixture and some of the crumbled bacon over the turnips. Drizzle with some of the remaining melted butter. Repeat layering turnips, flour mixture, bacon, and melted butter, ending with a layer of turnips. Pour the cream over the turnips.

Place the pie plate on a baking sheet. Spray a 9-inch square of aluminum foil with butter-flavored cooking spray and place, buttered-side down, on top of the turnips. Place a heavy 8- or 9-inch cast-iron skillet or pie plate on top and press firmly. Fill the pan with pie weights or dried beans and bake for 40 to 45 minutes, or until the bottom and sides are golden brown. (Check after 35 minutes, and if not browning, remove the foil and continue baking until the top is golden brown.)

Remove from the oven. With a spatula, loosen the turnip cake around the edges. Let cool for 5 minutes, then invert onto a serving plate and cut into wedges. Garnish with minced thyme and serve.

SERVES 6 TO 8

Sugar snap peas, also known as sugar peas or sugar snaps, are a sweet, crunchy cross between English peas and snow peas. Cooked very briefly to retain their color, crispness, and flavor, they are good in salads or as a side dish. Here they are cooked with green beans, butter beans, and baby lima beans, then topped with crisp bacon and slivers of almonds. Sugar snaps have strings on both seams that should be removed before eating. Just snap off a bit of the stem and pull gently down both sides.

MIXED BEANS WITH BACON AND ALMONDS

4 slices bacon

1 pound sugar snap peas, strings removed

1 pound green beans, trimmed

One 10-ounce package frozen butter beans

One 10-ounce package frozen lima beans

¼ cup slivered almonds

Salt and freshly ground pepper to taste

Olive oil for drizzling

In a small skillet over medium heat, cook the bacon until crisp. Using a slotted metal spatula, transfer to paper towels to drain.

In a large saucepan of salted boiling water, cook the sugar snap peas and green beans for 3 to 4 minutes. Drain, rinse in cold water, and drain again. Set aside. Cook the butter beans and lima beans in boiling salted water for about 8 minutes, or until tender. Drain. Combine the sugar snap peas and beans in a serving bowl, crumble the bacon on top, and sprinkle with the almonds. Season with salt and pepper and drizzle with a little olive oil.

SERVES 4 TO 6

Coast Road, near Doolin, County Clare.

Smithfield Horse Fair, Dublin.

Related to both onion and garlic, leeks look like giant scallions but are the mildest of all of the three. Leeks figure prominently in recipes of Celtic nations from the earliest times, especially as a flavoring in soups or stews. They are often served as a side dish, as in this gratin from Marigold Allen, hostess of the Beeches Country House, County Antrim.

LEEKS AU GRATIN

8 large leeks, white part only, halved
    lengthwise
½ cup heavy cream

2 cups shredded Cheddar cheese
Salt and freshly ground pepper to taste

½ cup fresh seasoned bread crumbs
    (page 30)

Preheat the oven to 350°F. Butter an ovenproof baking dish.

Cut each leek half into a 6-inch length and rinse well under running water. Cook in salted boiling water for 5 minutes, or until slightly tender. Drain.

Put the leeks, cut-side up, in the prepared baking dish, pour in the cream, and sprinkle with the cheese, salt, and pepper. Bake for 10 to 15 minutes, or until the cream has thickened and the cheese has melted.

Remove from the oven and preheat the broiler. Sprinkle the leeks with the bread crumbs, then place the dish under the broiler, 4 inches from the heat source, for 2 to 3 minutes, or until lightly browned.

SERVES 6

Margaret Browne, hostess of Ballymakeigh Country House, Killeagh, County Cork, poaches leeks first in stock before dressing them with a colorful pink peppercorn vinaigrette. She serves this dish with roast duck.

POACHED LEEKS WITH PINK PEPPERCORN DRESSING

8 to 10 large leeks, white part only, halved lengthwise

2 cups vegetable or chicken stock or canned low-salt chicken broth

PINK PEPPERCORN DRESSING:

2 tablespoons red wine vinegar

6 tablespoons olive oil

¼ cup fresh lemon juice

¼ cup pink peppercorns, lightly crushed

Freshly ground pepper to taste

Cut each leek half into a 6-inch length and rinse well under running water. In a large saucepan, bring the stock or broth to a boil. Add the leeks and cook for 10 minutes, or until tender. Drain. Transfer to a serving dish.

While the leeks are cooking, make the dressing. In a jar with a lid, combine the vinegar, olive oil, lemon juice, peppercorns, and pepper and shake well to blend. Pour the vinaigrette over the leeks while warm.

SERVES 6

Trinity College, Dublin.

SWEETS

Opposite, top: Baltimore, County Cork. Opposite, bottom: Dublin.

Bracks (from the Irish *breac,* meaning "speckled") are cakes studded with dried fruits and raisins that create a speckled effect when the cakes are sliced. Those made with yeast are called barmbracks, and those that use baking powder and fruit soaked in tea or cider are called tea bracks, or cider bracks. At Packies, one of the most renowned restaurants in the foodie haven of Kenmare, County Kerry, chef-owner Maura Foley uses barmbrack from Moriarty's Bakery to make this sumptuous bread and butter pudding that she serves with custard sauce. Prepare the pudding early on the day you plan to serve it.

MORIARTY'S BARMBRACK AND BUTTER PUDDING

Twelve 1-inch-thick slices Barmbrack (recipe follows), or other fruit-studded yeast bread (see note)

Room-temperature unsalted butter for spreading

2 teaspoons ground nutmeg

2⅔ cups half-and-half

2⅔ cups whole milk

6 eggs, beaten

¾ cup packed brown sugar

CUSTARD SAUCE:

1½ cups milk

5 egg yolks

½ cup granulated sugar

1 teaspoon vanilla extract

TO MAKE THE PUDDING: Generously butter an ovenproof baking dish. Spread each slice of barmbrack on one side with butter.

Cover the bottom of the dish with a layer of barmbrack, buttered-side up. Sprinkle with some of the nutmeg. Repeat layering until the barmbrack and nutmeg are used up.

In a medium saucepan, heat the half-and-half and milk to a simmer over medium heat. Whisk some of the hot milk mixture into the eggs, then return to the pan. Stir in the sugar, and pour over the layers of barmbrack, making sure each part is covered. Cover with plastic wrap and refrigerate for at least 4 hours or overnight.

Preheat the oven to 300°F. Put the baking dish in a roasting pan and add water to the roasting pan to come two-thirds of the way up the side of the baking dish. Bake for 40 to 45 minutes, or until the pudding is set and browned.

TO MAKE THE CUSTARD SAUCE: In a medium saucepan, bring the milk to a simmer over medium heat. In a large bowl, whisk the egg yolks and sugar together. Gradually whisk the hot milk into the yolk mixture, then return to the pan. Stir gently over medium heat for 6 to 8 minutes, or until custard thickens enough to coat the back of a spoon (do not boil). Transfer to a medium bowl, stir in the vanilla and let cool. Cover and refrigerate until cold, about 3 hours, or up to 24 hours.

To serve, spoon the pudding onto a serving plate and surround with custard sauce.

SERVES 6

NOTE: *If you don't have time to make the barmbrack and can't find a good fruit-studded bread, use layers of brioche or challah. Sprinkle with ½ cup golden raisins, ¼ cup candied lemon peel, and ¼ cup candied orange peel.*

Barmbrack

6 cups all-purpose flour

½ teaspoon Mixed Spice (recipe follows)

1 teaspoon salt

1 package active dry yeast

4 tablespoons granulated sugar

⅔ cup warm (105° to 115°F) water

1¼ cups warm (105° to 115°F) milk

¼ cup (½ stick) unsalted butter, melted

¼ cup currants

1 cup golden raisins

¼ cup candied lemon peel

1 egg beaten with 2 tablespoons water

In a food processor fitted with a paddle attachment, combine the flour, Mixed Spice, and salt. Pulse 2 to 3 times to combine. Add the yeast and sugar and pulse again. With the machine running, add the water, milk, and butter until the dough forms a ball. Continue processing to knead the dough for about 1 minute. Transfer the dough to a bowl, cover it with a damp cloth or plastic wrap coated with vegetable-oil cooking spray, and let rise in a warm place until doubled in size, 1 to 1½ hours.

Put the dough on a lightly floured work surface, flour your hands, and knead in the currants, raisins, and lemon peel. Return the dough to the bowl, cover again, and let it rise for 30 minutes, or until doubled in size.

Preheat the oven to 400°F. Generously grease a 10-inch round springform pan. Place the dough into the pan and let it rise again for 10 to 15 minutes. Brush the egg and water mixture over the top. Bake for 15 minutes. Cover with buttered foil, reduce the heat to 350°F, and bake for 40 to 45 minutes, or until the bread is golden and a skewer inserted into the center comes out clean. Turn out onto a wire rack and let cool completely. Run a knife around the inside edges of the pan and remove the metal ring.

MAKES 1 LOAF

Mixed Spice

In a spice grinder, combine 1 tablespoon coriander seeds; one 2-inch cinnamon stick, crushed; 1 teaspoon whole cloves; and 1 teaspoon allspice berries. Grind until powdery. Add 1 tablespoon ground nutmeg and 2 teaspoons ground ginger, and mix well. Pour into an airtight container and store in a cool, dark place.

MAKES ABOUT ⅓ CUP

The Old Bushmills Distillery in the village of Bushmills, County Antrim, is one of the area's chief attractions. In 1608, Sir Thomas Phillips was granted a "licence to distil," and the fine art of whiskey making continues there today on a much larger scale. The whiskeys produced there are counted among the finest in the world and are quite popular for drinking and cooking in the Bushmills Inn, a historic coaching stop not far from the distillery. Here, chef Eddie McGarvey laces a creamy custard sauce with Bushmills and uses it to top old-fashioned steamed marmalade puddings. If you like, use an Irish whiskey marmalade to enhance the flavor.

MARMALADE PUDDINGS WITH BUSHMILLS CUSTARD SAUCE

MARMALADE PUDDINGS:

¾ cup plus 1 tablespoon thick-cut orange marmalade

1½ cups (3 sticks) unsalted butter at room temperature

1½ cups superfine sugar

6 eggs, beaten

Grated zest of 2 oranges

3 cups self-rising flour

1 tablespoon ground allspice

BUSHMILLS CUSTARD SAUCE:

½ cup heavy cream

1 cup whole milk

5 egg yolks

½ cup superfine sugar

3 tablespoons Bushmills or other Irish whiskey

1 teaspoon vanilla extract

Orange segments and mint sprigs for garnish

TO MAKE THE PUDDINGS: Preheat the oven to 325°F. Generously grease six 4-ounce ramekins. Put 2 tablespoons of marmalade in the bottom of each.

In an electric mixer, combine the butter and sugar. Beat for 3 to 4 minutes, or until light and fluffy. Add the eggs, orange zest, and the remaining 1 tablespoon marmalade, then gradually beat in the flour and allspice. Spoon into the prepared ramekins.

Put the ramekins in a large baking pan and add hot water to the pan to come halfway up the side of the dishes. Cover the pan with waxed paper, then with aluminum foil, and prick the foil in 6 to 8 places. Bake for 25 minutes, or until the puddings are set and lightly browned. Remove from the oven.

TO MAKE THE CUSTARD SAUCE: In a heavy saucepan, combine the cream and milk and bring to a simmer over medium heat. In a large bowl, whisk the egg yolks and sugar together. Gradually whisk the hot milk into the yolks. Return to the pan and stir constantly over medium heat for 6 to 8 minutes, or until the custard thickens enough to coat the back of a spoon. Transfer to a bowl and whisk in the whiskey and vanilla. Set aside.

To serve, run a knife around the side of the ramekins and turn the puddings out onto serving plates. Spoon custard around the puddings and garnish with orange segments and a sprig of mint.

SERVES 6

Both the English and the Irish love this sweet, which is actually more like a cake than a pudding. The beauty of this sinfully rich dessert is that it can be made in any number of shapes to suit your serving needs: baked in a 12-cup bundt pan and cut into slices, baked in 12 bundt muffin pans and served as individual cakes, or baked in a rectangular pan and cut into squares. Regardless of the shape, the flavor of the pudding and the richness of the sauce is what makes this dessert special.

STICKY TOFFEE PUDDING

STICKY TOFFEE SAUCE:

4 cups heavy cream

2 cups packed dark brown sugar

½ cup (1 stick) unsalted butter

STICKY TOFFEE PUDDING:

1½ cups water

1¼ cups (8 ounces) dates, chopped and pitted

2 teaspoons baking soda

2½ cups all-purpose flour

2 teaspoons baking powder

1 cup (2 sticks) unsalted butter at room temperature

⅔ cup granulated sugar

4 large eggs

2 teaspoons vanilla extract

Sliced strawberries (optional)

TO MAKE THE SAUCE: In a medium saucepan, combine all the ingredients. Bring to a boil over medium heat, stirring constantly, then reduce heat to a simmer and cook, stirring frequently, for 5 to 7 minutes, or until the sauce has reduced to about 3½ cups. Set aside. To make ahead, cover and refrigerate for up to 12 hours, then reheat over low heat.

TO MAKE THE PUDDING: Preheat the oven to 350°F. Generously grease a 12-cup bundt pan or twelve 6-ounce bundt muffin pans.

In a medium saucepan, combine the water, dates, and baking soda. Bring to a boil over medium heat, then remove from the heat and set aside to cool completely. Combine the flour and baking powder in a medium bowl. Stir well to blend. Set aside.

In an electric mixer, beat the butter and sugar together for 3 to 4 minutes, or until light and fluffy. Beat in the eggs, one at a time, then the vanilla, and half of the flour mixture. Beat in all of the date mixture, then the remaining flour, until well blended. Pour or spoon into the prepared pan(s) and bake about 45 minutes for the bundt pan, 20 minutes for the bundt muffin pans, or until cake is golden brown. Pour half of the toffee sauce over the cake(s) and continue baking for about 15 minutes, or until a skewer inserted into the center comes out clean. Remove from the oven and let cool in the pan for 10 minutes. Invert onto plate(s).

To serve, cut the large cake into slices and drizzle toffee sauce over each slice. If serving individual cakes, put one in the center of a plate and spoon some sauce over. Garnish with sliced strawberries, if you wish.

SERVES 10 TO 12

Irish Honey

Honey is the only food we eat today that is made and consumed exactly the way it was ten thousand years ago. Pure, unadulterated natural food, it is made from nectar collected by bees. Monks and high priests of Ireland combined fermented honey with water to made mead, and warriors drank it for strength. Mead is also called "honeymoon wine" because it is believed to have powers of fertility and virility. The bride and groom at a medieval wedding drank mead for one full month after their wedding—hence the term *honeymoon*—and mead has long been used as a welcoming drink in Irish castles. Ireland's most popular brand is Bunratty Meade, produced at the Bunratty Winery behind the Folk Park in County Clare.

Today, Irish cooks often use honey and mead to add sweetness to dishes ranging from red cabbage to Cornish hens, and the Milleeven Honey company in County Kilkenny sells honey flavored with Irish spirits, as well as fresh berries preserved in honey for use as a topping for ice cream, puddings, and cakes. Other brands include Molaga, produced in Timoleague, West Cork, and Boyne Valley honey, produced in County Louth. See Resources (page 161) for details on where to find Irish honey.

Bandon, County Cork.

A statue of Dublin poet Patrick Kavanagh
on the banks of the Grand Canal, Dublin.

A favorite way for Irish women to temper the strong taste of Guinness is to add a dash of black currant liqueur or brandy. At the Patrick Kavanagh Dining Room at Dublin's Hibernian Hotel, this idea finds its way into a soufflé that capitalizes on the intense flavor of Guinness and the sweetness of black currants. If black currants aren't available, you can substitute black-berries.

GUINNESS SOUFFLÉS WITH BLACK CURRANT COULIS

BLACK CURRANT COULIS:

½ cup superfine sugar

2 cups (8 ounces) fresh black currants or blackberries

¼ cup crème de cassis liqueur

¼ cup water

1 tablespoon light corn syrup

SOUFFLÉS:

3 cups whole milk

8 egg yolks

⅔ cup plus ½ cup superfine sugar

1½ cups all-purpose flour

2 cups Guinness stout

5 egg whites

Confectioners' sugar

TO MAKE THE COULIS: In a blender or food processor, combine all the ingredients and process for 20 to 30 seconds, or until smooth. Transfer to a small saucepan and bring to a boil over medium heat. Cook, stirring constantly, for 2 to 3 minutes, or until thickened. Strain into a clean bowl and refrigerate.

TO MAKE THE SOUFFLÉS: Preheat the oven to 300°F. Butter and flour six 4-ounce ramekins.

In a medium saucepan, bring the milk to a boil over medium heat. Whisk in the egg yolks, the ⅔ cup sugar, and the flour. Remove from heat and let cool completely. In a small saucepan, bring the Guinness to a boil over medium heat and cook for 8 to 10 minutes, or until reduced to ½ cup. Let cool slightly, then stir into the cream mixture.

In the bowl of an electric mixer, beat the egg whites until foamy, then gradually beat in the ½ cup sugar until soft peaks form. Stir one-fourth of the whites into the Guinness mixture to lighten it. Fold in the remaining whites until blended. Spoon the soufflé mixture into the prepared ramekins and place in a baking pan. Add enough hot water to the pan to come halfway up the side of the dishes. Bake for 12 to 15 minutes, or until set.

To serve, run a knife around the side of the ramekins to loosen the soufflés, then lift out and place on serving plates. Spoon the coulis around the soufflés and dust with confectioners' sugar. Serve warm.

SERVES 6

Blueberries, relatively new to Ireland as a cultivated crop, are a bit like big brothers to the tiny fraughans, or bilberries, that grow wild and ripen on the mountainsides in August. Several blueberry farms are now in operation, the largest, Derryvilla Farm near Portarlington, County Offaly, being responsible for almost 90 percent of Ireland's blueberry harvest. Chefs in some of the country's top restaurants have been experimenting with blueberries in tarts, puddings, and sauces. Chef Robbie Millar of Shanks Restaurant, near Bangor, County Down, created these sensuous, silky crèmes brûlées laden with blueberries and deliciously scented with lemon balm, lemon juice, lemon zest, and lemongrass.

LEMON AND BLUEBERRY CRÈMES BRÛLÉES

1¾ cups (8 ounces) fresh or frozen blueberries

1 tablespoon granulated sugar

1 teaspoon cornstarch

2 cups heavy cream

2 teaspoons vanilla extract

½ stalk lemongrass, white part only, peeled and chopped

1 sprig lemon balm, chopped (see note)

Grated zest of 1 lemon

2 tablespoons fresh lemon juice

5 egg yolks

¼ cup superfine sugar

1½ tablespoons packed brown sugar

In a small saucepan, combine half of the blueberries with the granulated sugar. Cook over medium-low heat, uncovered, for 5 minutes, or until the juices begin to run. Sprinkle the cornstarch over the blueberries and cook for 2 to 3 minutes, or until the mixture begins to thicken. Remove from the heat and stir in the remaining berries. Divide the berry mixture among six 4-ounce buttered ramekins and set aside.

In a small saucepan, combine the cream, vanilla, lemongrass, lemon balm, lemon zest, and lemon juice and bring gently to a boil over medium-low heat. Remove from the heat and let sit for 1 hour.

Preheat the oven to 325°F. Strain the custard into a clean saucepan and heat over medium heat. Do not let it boil. In a medium bowl, whisk the egg yolks and superfine sugar together. Gradually whisk in the hot cream. Spoon into the prepared ramekins (the blueberries may float to the top, but they will sink again)

and place in a baking pan. Add enough hot water to the pan to come halfway up the side of the dishes. Bake for 40 to 45 minutes, or until the custards are set. Remove from the oven and let cool in the baking pan for 15 minutes. Remove from the pan and let cool completely. Cover with plastic wrap and refrigerate for at least 1 hour or up to 24 hours.

Preheat the broiler. Sprinkle each custard with about 1 teaspoon brown sugar. Place under the broiler 4 inches from the heat source for 1 to 2 minutes, or use a kitchen blowtorch and move the flame constantly over the surface until the sugar melts, bubbles, and lightly browns.

SERVES 6

NOTE: *If you can't find lemongrass, increase the lemon juice to 3 tablespoons. A good substitute for the lemon balm is ¼ teaspoon lemon oil or ½ teaspoon minced fresh mint.*

Sweet Irish Creams

Irish cream liqueurs are made from a blend of two of Ireland's greatest treasures: the cream from its rich dairy pastures and the spirits from its finest distilleries. Baileys Irish Cream, the first of the bunch, was launched in 1974 after the makers discovered the secret that would prevent cream from separating after being blended with neutral spirits, Irish whiskey, and natural flavors. Steeped in Irish history and lore, it was named after a Dublin pub called the Bailey, a favorite haunt of James Joyce. Its bottle design is based on an old Irish whiskey brand, Red Breast.

Some say that a whiskey-flavored cream like Baileys is based from the tradition west of Ireland: stirring fresh cream into Irish whiskey for sipping. Its popularity has grown throughout Ireland and the world, and today there are several brands of Irish cream liqueur, including Carolans, Emmets, Saint Brendan's, and O'Mara's.

Locke's Distillery, Kilbeggan, County Westmeath.

Irish playwright George Bernard Shaw loved brown soda bread and once said of it: "Remember that brown bread is a good familiar creature and worth more than his weight in flesh." Chances are Mr. Shaw never imagined this homey loaf as an ingredient in dishes ranging from soups to crumble to crèmes brûlées. Because the bread doesn't keep well, such uses solve the problem of what to do with leftover bread. Ambitious cooks might even want to bake an extra loaf, slice it, and freeze it for these occasions. Chefs like Chris King of the Woodstock Hotel, Ennis, County Clare, use brown bread to full advantage in this whiskey-flavored, ultra-sweet dessert. Pair it with Black Currant Coulis (page 131).

JAMESON AND BROWN BREAD CRÈMES BRÛLÉES

BROWN SODA BREAD:

3 cups all-purpose flour

1½ cups whole-wheat flour

½ cup quick-cooking Irish oatmeal, preferably McCann's brand, plus more for sprinkling

⅓ cup steel-cut Irish oatmeal, preferably McCann's brand

2½ teaspoons baking soda

⅓ cup granulated sugar

4 tablespoons cold unsalted butter, cut into small pieces

2¼ cups buttermilk

CRÈMES BRÛLÉES:

½ cup packed brown sugar

Two 1-inch-thick slices brown soda bread (recipe above), broken into small pieces

½ cup superfine sugar

4 egg yolks

1 cup heavy cream

1 teaspoon vanilla extract

3 tablespoons Jameson Irish whiskey or similar brand

1½ tablespoons packed brown sugar

TO MAKE THE BROWN SODA BREAD: Preheat the oven to 425°F. Lightly dust the surface of a baking sheet with flour.

In a large bowl, stir the dry ingredients together. Using a pastry cutter or your fingers, work in the butter until the mixture resembles coarse crumbs. Make a well in the center and gradually stir in the buttermilk until blended.

Turn the dough onto a lightly floured work surface and knead for about 1 minute. Shape the dough into a ball and place it in the center of the prepared baking sheet. Flatten the dough into a mound about 1½ inches thick. With a sharp knife that has been dipped in flour, make a cross through the center of the bread so that it will easily break into quarters when baked (do not cut all the way through). Sprinkle a little oatmeal over the top.

Bake for 30 to 35 minutes, or until the bread is nicely browned and a skewer inserted into the center comes out clean. Check after 20 minutes, and if browning too quickly, reduce heat to 350°F.

TO MAKE THE CRÈMES BRÛLÉES: Preheat the broiler. In a small bowl, combine the brown sugar and bread pieces. Spread the mixture out on a baking sheet and put it under the broiler 6 inches from the heat source. Cook, stirring once or twice, for 5 minutes, or until the sugar melts and caramelizes. Remove from the oven. Scrape the caramelized crumbs back into the bowl to let cool and harden. Put the mixture into a self-sealing plastic bag and using a rolling pin, crush it into fine crumbs. Spoon the crumbs equally into six 4-ounce ramekins. Set aside.

In a small bowl, whisk the superfine sugar and egg yolks together until light and fluffy. In a saucepan, bring the cream to a boil over medium heat. Stir in the vanilla and whiskey. Gradually whisk the cream mixture into the egg mixture, then return to the pan and cook for 3 to 4 minutes, or until it thickens and coats the back of a spoon. Spoon into the crumb-filled ramekins and refrigerate for 4 to 5 hours, or until the custard is set.

Preheat the broiler. Sprinkle each custard with about 1 teaspoon brown sugar. Place under the broiler 4 inches from the heat source for 1 to 2 minutes, or use a kitchen blowtorch and move the flame constantly over the surface until the sugar melts, bubbles, and lightly browns.

SERVES 6

Madeira cake, a simple pound cake sometimes sprinkled with candied lemon peel, is so-called because it was traditionally served with a glass of Madeira. Here it substitutes for sponge cake as the base for a deceptively simple, yet impressive Irish version of baked Alaska. The recipe is featured in *Baileys Pure Indulgence,* a cookbook published by Baileys.

BAILEYS BAKED ALASKAS ON MADEIRA CAKE

MADEIRA CAKE:

½ cup (1 stick) unsalted butter

½ cup granulated sugar

4 eggs

2 cups self-rising flour

Grated zest and juice of 1 lemon

2 tablespoons candied lemon peel

2 tablespoons superfine sugar

BAKED ALASKAS:

3 to 4 tablespoons ground almonds

4 scoops Häagen-Dazs Baileys Irish
   Cream ice cream

3 to 4 tablespoons brandy

4 egg whites

Pinch of cream of tartar

½ cup superfine sugar

Confectioners' sugar for dusting

TO MAKE THE CAKE: Preheat the oven to 350°F. Grease and flour a 9-by-5-inch loaf pan.

In an electric mixer, cream the butter and granulated sugar together until light and fluffy. Add 2 of the eggs, one at a time, beating well after each addition. Add ½ cup of the flour and beat thoroughly. Add the remaining eggs, the remaining 1½ cups flour, lemon zest and juice, and beat again.

Spoon the batter into the prepared pan and bake for 30 minutes. Press the candied lemon peel into the top of the cake, sprinkle with the superfine sugar, and bake 30 minutes longer, or until the cake is lightly browned and a skewer inserted in the center comes out clean. Remove from the oven and let cool on a rack. Remove the cake from the pan.

TO MAKE THE BAKED ALASKAS: Spread the almonds out on a plate. Roll each scoop of ice cream in the almonds, place on a baking sheet, and freeze for 30 minutes. Cut the cake into four ½-inch-thick slices and trim to make each slice a square. Drizzle with brandy. Place the slices a few inches apart on a baking sheet, put a scoop of ice cream in the center of each slice, and return to the freezer.

Preheat the oven to 450°F. In a large bowl, beat the egg whites and cream of tartar until soft peaks form. Beat in the superfine sugar, 1 tablespoon at a time, until stiff, glossy peaks form. With a rubber spatula, spread the meringue over the ice cream to cover. Bake for 5 minutes, or until the meringue is lightly browned.

To serve, place a baked Alaska on each plate and dust with confectioners' sugar.

SERVES 4

All cooks have a favorite recipe for a chocolate dessert, and flourless, or "fallen," chocolate cake—the kind that simply oozes onto the plate—is one of the most popular. I love this one from home cook Phyl Clarke of Dublin, who serves it with chocolate shavings and slightly warmed seasonal fruits. Clarke's recipe first appeared as a reader's submission in Dublin's *Food & Wine* magazine.

CHOCOLATE MOUSSE CAKE

9 ounces bittersweet chocolate, chopped

½ cup plus 2 tablespoons superfine sugar

½ cup (1 stick) plus 2 tablespoons unsalted butter

½ cup ground almonds

5 eggs, separated

Confectioners' sugar for dusting

Chocolate shavings and seasonal fruits for garnish (optional)

Preheat the oven to 350°F. Generously butter and flour a 10-inch springform pan.

In a medium saucepan, combine the chocolate, superfine sugar, and butter. Cook over low heat until the butter and chocolate melt. Stir until smooth. Remove from the heat and add the almonds. Stir in the egg yolks, one at a time.

In a large bowl, beat the egg whites until stiff, glossy peaks form. Stir 2 to 3 spoonfuls of the egg whites into the chocolate mixture to lighten it, then gently fold in the rest until well blended. Turn into the prepared pan and bake for 35 to 40 minutes, or until the top is firm. The cake will rise, form a crust, then fall again. Remove from the oven and let cool completely on a wire rack. Run a knife around the inside edges of the pan and remove the metal ring.

To serve, dust the cake with the confectioners' sugar and garnish with chocolate shavings and fresh fruit, if you wish.

SERVES 8 TO 10

A Taste of West Cork

There are many well-known examples of traditional Irish fare that have a distinct local character. A number of Ireland's finest foods—Clonakilty puddings, Bantry Bay mussels, Ballydehob duck, farmhouse cheeses—have their origins in West Cork, a region famed for its natural beauty, unique character, and culture.

Over the last few decades, the area has become synonymous with award-winning cuisine as well. To raise the profile of locally produced goods, a branding initiative, spearheaded by West Cork Leader (a cooperative food society) in conjunction with Fuschia Brands (a local food distributor), was designed to profile foods that reflect local characteristics and the richness of the heritage, culture, and landscape. The organization regularly offers recipes that draw inspiration from the work of local producers and reflect modern culinary trends. Examples can be found throughout *The New Irish Table*.

Mannings Emporium, Ballylickey, County Cork.

West Cork.

The **Two Dog** Café in Clifden, County Galway, is an eclectic mix of homespun cooking and cyberspace technology. Not only does it serve great food, coffee, and wines, it provides full Internet access and services. Hosts Jon Lemon and Jane Hackett provide the bytes and bites respectively in Clifden, capital of the Connemara region.

ORANGE ALMOND CAKE

2 large oranges

1 cup superfine sugar

1 cup ground almonds

6 large eggs

1 teaspoon baking powder

ORANGE SYRUP:

6 cardamom pods

2 cups fresh orange juice

½ cup superfine sugar

1 cinnamon stick

Confectioners' sugar for dusting

¾ cup crème fraîche (page 105)

Preheat the oven to 350°F. Grease and flour a 10-inch springform pan.

With a fork, pierce the oranges in 2 or 3 places. Put them in a microwave-safe bowl and microwave on high for 4 minutes, or until soft. Let cool for 10 to 15 minutes. Cut the oranges into quarters and remove any seeds.

Put the oranges, including the skin and any juice, in a food processor and process for 2 to 3 minutes, or until smooth. Add the superfine sugar and process for 30 seconds, or until smooth. Add the almonds, eggs, and baking powder and process for 1 minute more, or until well blended. Turn into the prepared pan and bake for 30 to 35 minutes, or until the top is firm. The cake will rise, form a crust, then fall again. Remove from the oven and let cool completely on a wire rack. Run a knife around the inside edges of the pan and remove the metal ring.

TO MAKE THE SYRUP: Crush the cardamom pods to release the seeds. In a medium saucepan, combine the cardamom seeds, orange juice, superfine sugar, and cinnamon stick and bring to a boil over medium heat. Reduce the heat to a simmer and cook for 8 to 10 minutes, or until slightly thickened. Remove from the heat, strain the syrup, and let cool.

To serve, dust the cake with the confectioners' sugar. Serve with orange syrup and a spoonful of crème fraîche.

SERVES 8 TO 10

Sisters Marog O'Brien and Kay Harte operate two of County Cork's best-loved eating places: the Farmgate Restaurant and Country Store, established in 1983 in Midleton, and the Farmgate Café and Restaurant, which opened in October 1994 in the English Market, Cork City. Both serve luscious, homespun meals—sandwiches, salads, soups, stews—and highly acclaimed desserts, like pear and almond tart, fruit-filled pastries, and carrot cake, which are displayed atop a grand piano in the restaurant and surrounded by bowls of thick whipped cream. This traditional carrot cake comes with a velvety cream cheese icing.

FARMGATE CARROT CAKE

½ cup granulated sugar

⅔ cup sunflower oil

3 eggs

1 cup all-purpose flour

1 teaspoon baking soda

2 teaspoons ground cinnamon

½ teaspoon ground nutmeg

½ teaspoon ground cloves

¾ cup grated carrots

1 cup chopped walnuts

½ cup golden raisins

One 8-ounce can crushed pineapple, drained

CREAM CHEESE ICING:

½ cup (1 stick) unsalted butter at room temperature

½ cup (4 ounces) cream cheese at room temperature

1 cup confectioners' sugar, sifted

Preheat the oven to 325°F. Grease an 8-by-8-inch square pan.

In an electric mixer, combine the sugar, oil, and eggs. Beat until smooth. Sift the flour, baking soda, cinnamon, nutmeg, and cloves together. Add to the oil mixture and beat until well combined. Stir in the carrots, walnuts, raisins, and pineapple. Pour into the prepared pan and bake for 45 to 55 minutes, or until the top is browned and a skewer inserted in the center comes out clean. Remove from the oven and let cool on a wire rack. Remove the cake from the pan and transfer to a serving plate for icing.

TO MAKE THE CREAM CHEESE ICING: In an electric mixer, combine the butter and cream cheese and beat until smooth. Gradually mix in the confectioners' sugar and beat until smooth. Spread the icing over the cake and cut into squares to serve.

SERVES 8 TO 10

Midleton, County Cork.

Street market, Dublin.

Grace Neill's is listed in the *Guinness Book of Records* as the oldest bar in Ireland. It first opened in 1611 as the King's Arms in Donaghadee, County Down, and was renamed in the nineteenth century for its former landlady, a woman who reportedly greeted all visitors to the inn with a welcoming kiss in between puffs on her clay pipe. Today, guests at Grace Neill's, which includes a bar and restaurant named Bistro Bistro, often report "sightings" of the Victorian woman, which some attribute to one too many servings of these Guinness-spiked brownies.

GRACE NEILL'S CHOCOLATE AND GUINNESS BROWNIES

4 eggs

¾ cup superfine sugar

8 ounces bittersweet chocolate, chopped

4 ounces white chocolate, chopped

6 tablespoons unsalted butter

¾ cup all-purpose flour

¾ cup cocoa

1¼ cups Guinness stout

Confectioners' sugar for dusting

Preheat the oven to 375°F. Butter an 8-by-8-inch square pan.

In an electric mixer, combine the eggs and superfine sugar. Beat until light and fluffy.

In a medium saucepan, over medium heat, melt the bittersweet chocolate, white chocolate, and butter, stirring until smooth. Remove from heat and beat into the egg mixture.

Sift the flour and cocoa together and beat into the chocolate mixture. Whisk in the Guinness.

Pour into the prepared pan and bake for 20 to 25 minutes, or until a skewer inserted in the center comes out almost clean. Remove from the oven and let cool on a wire rack. To serve, dust the cake with confectioners' sugar and cut into squares.

SERVES 8 TO 10

Avoca Handweavers is one of Ireland's most popular places to shop for Irish crafts, clothing, and food. With locations in the country's most popular tourist destinations (Wicklow, the Ring of Kerry, Bunratty), you might expect the food at these places to be typical roadside fare. Not so. This luscious pear-filled, pear-topped tart with a crunchy caramel crust is one of the desserts you might find.

SPICY PEAR TART

1 cup packed light brown sugar	1 cup superfine sugar	½ teaspoon salt
½ cup (1 stick) unsalted butter	1 teaspoon baking powder	2 eggs
4 pears, peeled and cored	1 teaspoon ground ginger	⅔ cup canola oil
1½ cups all-purpose flour	2 teaspoons ground cinnamon	Whipped cream for serving (optional)

Preheat the oven to 300°F. Wrap a 10-inch round springform pan in 2 layers of aluminum foil to prevent leaking. In a small saucepan, combine the brown sugar and butter over medium heat. Cook, stirring constantly, for about 5 minutes, until the butter and sugar caramelize. Pour the caramel into the prepared springform pan. Set aside.

Using the large holes of a box grater, shred one of the pears. Slice the remaining pears. In a medium bowl, combine the flour, superfine sugar, baking powder, ginger, cinnamon, and salt. In a separate bowl, beat the eggs and oil together. Stir in the shredded pear. Stir the dry ingredients into the egg mixture. Pour over the caramel base. Arrange the sliced pears on top in a concentric circle, starting from the center. Bake for 1 hour and 15 minutes, or until the base bubbles and the pears are soft. Remove from the oven and let cool slightly in the pan. Remove the sides of the pan. Slice and serve with whipped cream, if you wish.

SERVES 8 TO 10

Mills Inn, Ballyvourney, County Cork.

This "cobbler," from chef Sandy Plumb of the McCausland Hotel in Belfast, County Antrim, is actually more like a streudel, or what the Irish call a Swiss roll, with the apples rolled up inside.

ARMAGH APPLE COBBLER

1 cup (2 sticks) cold unsalted butter

1 cup granulated sugar

1 cup water

1½ cups self-rising flour

⅓ cup milk

2 Granny Smith apples, peeled, cored, and diced

1 teaspoon ground cinnamon

Whipped cream for serving (optional)

Preheat the oven to 350°F. Melt ½ cup of the butter and spread it in the bottom of a 9-by-13-inch baking pan.

In a medium saucepan, combine the sugar and water. Cook over medium heat for 1 to 2 minutes, or until the sugar dissolves and becomes syrupy. Set aside.

Cut up the remaining ½ cup butter. In a food processor, combine the flour and butter. Process for 20 to 30 seconds, or until the mixture resembles coarse crumbs. Add the milk and process for 1 minute, or until the dough comes together. Turn the dough out onto a lightly floured work surface and knead for 2 to 3 minutes, or until smooth. Form it into a ball, then wrap it in plastic wrap and refrigerate for 30 minutes. Remove the dough

from the refrigerator 20 minutes before rolling. Roll the dough out to a 10-by-12-inch rectangle.

In a large bowl, combine the apples and cinnamon. Sprinkle the apples over the dough and roll up, beginning with the long side. Press the edges to seal. Cut the roll into 12 slices, each about 1-inch thick. Arrange the slices in the prepared baking dish and pour the sugar syrup around and over the slices. (This will look like too much liquid, but the crust will absorb it during baking.) Bake for 40 to 45 minutes, or until golden brown. Remove from the oven and let cool for 15 minutes. Serve 2 slices per person, with whipped cream, if you wish.

SERVES 6

Preston House is a beautiful ivy-clad former schoolhouse located in the heritage town of Abbeyleix, County Laois. In addition to housing an outstanding restaurant, Preston House Café, accommodations are offered as well, both under the direction of the Dowling family. Try these lovely tartlets, from host Allison Dowling, with whipped cream or vanilla ice cream.

BLUEBERRY AND APPLE TARTLETS

PASTRY:

3 cups all-purpose flour

1 cup (2 sticks) cold unsalted butter, cut into pieces

½ cup superfine sugar

1 egg beaten with 1 tablespoon water

FILLING:

2 pounds tart apples, peeled, cored, and chopped

½ cup granulated sugar

3 cups fresh or frozen blueberries

1 egg, beaten

¾ cup half-and-half

Whipped cream or vanilla ice cream for serving (optional)

TO MAKE THE PASTRY: In a food processor, combine the flour, butter, and sugar. Process for 20 to 30 seconds, or until the mixture resembles coarse crumbs. Add the egg mixture and process for 1 minute, or until the dough comes together. Turn the dough out onto a lightly floured work surface, form it into a disk, then wrap in plastic wrap and refrigerate for 1 hour. Remove the dough from the refrigerator 20 minutes before rolling. Cut it in half.

Preheat the oven to 350°F. On a lightly floured work surface, roll each dough half out to a ¼-inch thickness. Using a 4-inch-diameter biscuit or cookie cutter, cut out 12 rounds of pastry and press each piece into a loose-bottom tart pan. Line each with aluminum foil and fill with pie weights or dried beans. Place on a baking sheet and bake for 20 minutes or until set. Remove the foil and weights and let cool.

TO MAKE THE FILLING: In a large saucepan, combine the apples with ¼ cup of the sugar. Cook for 5 to 7 minutes, or until the apples are soft. Remove from heat and let cool. In a separate saucepan, combine the remaining ¼ cup sugar with the blueberries and cook over medium heat for 3 to 4 minutes, or until the blueberries and sugar are syrupy. Remove from heat and let cool. Combine the apples and blueberries.

Spoon the apples and blueberries into the tartlet shells. In a small bowl, whisk the egg and half-and-half together. Spoon over the fruit and bake for 15 to 20 minutes, or until set. Serve warm with whipped cream or vanilla ice cream, if you wish.

SERVES 12

This tart is adapted from a recipe in *A Taste of West Cork* (see page 139). Neither a traditional tart nor crumble, it's an interesting combination of both and is baked in a free-form, rustic style.

RUSTIC APPLE TART WITH HAZELNUT CRUMBLE

PASTRY:

1 cup all-purpose flour

⅛ teaspoon granulated sugar

Pinch of salt

6 tablespoons cold unsalted butter, cut into pieces

2½ tablespoons ice water

FILLING:

2 tablespoons all-purpose flour

1 pound Granny Smith apples, peeled, cored, and diced

3 tablespoons unsalted butter

½ cup granulated sugar

1 teaspoon ground cinnamon

2 tablespoons unsalted butter, melted

CRUMBLE:

⅓ cup granulated sugar

⅓ cup packed brown sugar

⅓ cup all-purpose flour

⅓ cup hazelnuts

4 tablespoons unsalted butter

Whipped cream or Bushmills Custard Sauce (page 127) for serving (optional)

TO MAKE THE PASTRY: In a food processor, combine the flour, sugar, salt, and butter. Process for 20 to 30 seconds, or until the mixture resembles coarse crumbs. Add the water and process for 1 minute, or until the dough comes together. Turn the dough out onto a lightly floured work surface, form it into a ball, then wrap it in plastic wrap and refrigerate for 1 hour. Remove the dough from the refrigerator 20 minutes before rolling.

Preheat the oven to 400°F. Line a baking sheet with parchment paper. On a lightly floured work surface, roll the dough out to an 11-inch round. Transfer to the prepared baking sheet.

TO MAKE THE FILLING: Sprinkle the flour over the crust, leaving a 1½-inch border. In a medium saucepan, combine the apples, 3 tablespoons butter, and sugar. Sprinkle with the cinnamon and cook over medium heat for 3 to 5 minutes, or until the apples are slightly tender. Remove from the heat and let cool for 10 minutes. Spread the apple mixture into the center of the pastry, leaving a 1½-inch border. Fold the pastry border up over the fruit, making a pleated border as you go. Brush the crust with the melted butter.

TO MAKE THE CRUMBLE: In a food processor, combine all the ingredients and pulse 2 to 3 times, or until the mixture resembles coarse crumbs. Do not overprocess. Sprinkle over the apple mixture and bake for 40 to 50 minutes, or until the crumble is lightly browned and the apples are tender. (Some juices will leak onto the parchment paper.) Serve warm with whipped cream or custard sauce, if you wish.

SERVES 6 TO 8

One of Italy's great gifts to the dessert world is zabaglione, a heavenly combination of egg yolks, sugar, and Marsala wine whisked over simmering water to a pale yellow froth. In France and other parts of the world the sauce is called sabayon, and now there's a distinctly Irish version made with Irish Mist liqueur, a blend of four distilled spirits, Irish honey, and exotic herbs.

GRATIN OF SUMMER FRUITS WITH IRISH MIST SABAYON

SABAYON:

4 egg yolks

¼ cup superfine sugar

3 tablespoons Irish Mist liqueur

¾ cup dry white wine

2 teaspoons fresh lemon juice

GRATIN:

¾ cup fresh or frozen raspberries

1 cup fresh strawberries, hulled and sliced

1 cup fresh or frozen blackberries or blueberries

Confectioners' sugar for dusting

Mint springs for garnish

TO MAKE THE SABAYON: In a double boiler, combine all the ingredients. Place over simmering, not boiling, water and whisk for 8 to 10 minutes, or until thick, pale, and creamy.

TO MAKE THE GRATIN: Preheat the broiler. Divide the fruit among six 8-ounce ovenproof bowls. Spoon the sabayon over the top and brown lightly under the broiler 4 inches from the heat source for about 2 minutes, or use a kitchen blowtorch and move flame constantly over the surface until the top is lightly browned. Dust with confectioners' sugar and garnish with sprigs of mint.

SERVES 6

From Shannon to San Francisco
Irish Coffee Comes to America

Irish coffee may have been invented in Ireland, but it was introduced to the world at the Buena Vista Café in San Francisco.

The year was 1943, and chef-barman Joe Sheridan decided that a blend of cream, hot coffee, and Irish whiskey would make a perfect welcoming drink for cold and weary passengers arriving at Foynes, County Limerick, from the United States on the Flying Boats, the first transatlantic passenger planes. He wanted the drink to be warm and welcoming, Irish in character, and sophisticated enough to appeal to international travelers. After many experiments over a number of years, including the addition of sugar, Joe Sheridan finally came up with the recipe for what would become the quintessential Irish drink. When Shannon International Airport opened in 1947, Irish coffee became its official beverage.

In the early 1950s, *San Francisco Chronicle* journalist Stan Delaplane enjoyed an Irish coffee at Shannon and introduced it to America at his favorite watering hole, the Buena Vista Café near Fisherman's Wharf. Although Delaplane's demonstration drink was described as a "muddy looking affair" and the cream wouldn't float, the answer to the sinking cream was eventually sorted out by a local dairy farmer who suggested that the cream should be beaten until just lightly thickened rather than fully whipped. Irish coffee soon became the drink of San Francisco, and since its introduction in 1952, more than 15 million have been served at the popular restaurant alone, and millions more elsewhere.

Here is Joe Sheridan's original recipe, which is still used at the Buena Vista: Heat a stemmed heatproof goblet by running it under very hot water. Pour in 1 jigger of Irish whiskey. Add 3 cubes sugar and fill the goblet with strong black coffee to within 1 inch of the brim. Stir to dissolve the sugar. Top off with lightly whipped cream. Do not stir after adding the cream, as the true flavor is obtained by drinking the hot mixture through the cream.

Killarney, County Kerry.

Poached pears are a lovely dessert on their own, but when poached in Bunratty Meade, a honey-based white wine made in Bunratty, County Clare, they take on a new flavor dimension (see note). This recipe, from the Celt's Banquet in Dublin, is one of several dishes prepared there that have a distinctive Celtic influence.

PEARS POACHED IN MEAD

1¼ cups plus 2 tablespoons Bunratty Meade

¾ cup granulated sugar

½ cup water

2 to 3 cinnamon sticks

Stripped zest of 1 orange

6 firm Bosc or Bartlett pears, peeled, stem intact

1¼ cups heavy cream

In a large saucepan, combine the 1¼ cups mead, the granulated sugar, water, cinnamon sticks, and orange zest. Bring to a boil over medium heat. Cook for 6 to 8 minutes, or until the sugar dissolves and the mixture becomes syrupy. Reduce heat to a simmer, add the pears, cover, and cook for 25 to 35 minutes, or until the pears are tender. Remove from heat and let the pears let cool in the poaching liquid.

In an electric mixer, combine the 2 tablespoons mead with the cream and beat until thick. To serve, pour some of the poaching liquid into the center of each serving plate, stand a pear on top, and add a spoonful of the whipped cream.

SERVES 6

NOTE: *Like Irish whiskey, which is spelled with an "e" to differentiate it from Scotch whisky, Bunratty Meade is spelled with an "e" to designate it as a specific brand of mead.*

O'Brien's Farm Shop, County Tipperary.

ABBEY BLUE BRIE CHEESE

Produced by the Hyland family in Ballacolla, County Laois, Abbey is a mild blue Brie, with a thick white rind that holds the soft cheese paste.

BACON, LOIN OF

Much like smoked pork shoulder in taste, a loin of bacon is a thick slab of pork taken from the belly of a pig. It is the meat used in the traditional Irish dish known as bacon and cabbage.

BLACK PUDDING

Black pudding, the most famous of which is made in Clonakilty, County Cork, is a sausage made of ground pork, spices, oatmeal, and pork blood, which gives it its distinctive color. Black pudding is traditionally served as part of an Irish breakfast, although today it is also used as an ingredient in salads, terrines, and meat dishes.

BLARNEY CHEESE

A Kerrygold brand of semisoft and part-skimmed cheese. Reminiscent of a young Gouda in both flavor and texture.

GLOSSARY

BACON, TRADITIONAL IRISH

Irish bacon is less fatty than American-style bacon and less crispy when cooked. When sliced thin and served as part of an Irish breakfast, the bacon strips are known as *rashers*.

BAILEYS IRISH CREAM

Made from Irish whiskey, double cream, neutral spirits, and natural flavors, Baileys Irish Cream was the first of several cream liqueurs produced in Ireland.

BANGERS

Bangers are sausages made of ground pork and bread crumbs. They are used in coddle, a casserole of sausage and potatoes, or served with mashed potatoes. Bangers are an integral part of an Irish breakfast.

BARMBRACK

A fruit-studded yeast bread, this was once the traditional dessert served on Halloween, the eve of the Celtic New Year.

BOILIE CHEESE

Made in County Cavan, Boilie is a soft cheese made from both cow's and goat's milk. It is rolled into little balls, then bottled in sunflower oil seasoned with pink peppercorns, fresh herbs, and garlic.

BOXTY

A traditional potato pancake, made with a combination of grated raw potatoes and mashed potatoes.

CASHEL BLUE CHEESE

Produced by Jane and Louis Grubb in Fethard, County Tipperary, Cashel Blue has been made from the milk of pedigreed Friesian cows since 1986. It is best eaten at around four months old, when it turns a rich yellow and develops a buttery flavor. Cashel is Ireland's best known blue cheese.

CHAMP

A traditional potato dish made with mashed potatoes and green onions.

CIDER

Pressed from apples, cider may be "sweet," or unfermented, or fermented, when it is called hard cider. Femented cider has always been a popular drink in Ireland. Bulmers, Strongbow, Linden Village, and Magners are popular brands available in bottles and on draught.

COLCANNON

A traditional potato dish made with mashed potatoes and cabbage or kale.

COOLEA CHEESE

This Irish cheese, made with the milk from a small herd farmed on the hillsides of Coolea, County Cork, has its origins in Dutch Gouda. Only summer milk is used in production, and the cheese is matured from six to fourteen months.

COOLEENEY CHEESE

The Maher family has produced this cheese on their farm in Thurles, County Tipperary, since 1986. It is made from high-quality raw milk from their own herd in the style of a Camembert, but the flavor is robust with tastes of oak and mushrooms.

DIGESTIVE BISCUITS

Semi-sweet crackers often served with tea.

DUBLINER CHEESE

A Kerrygold brand of cheese with a hard texture, not unlike a Cheddar, but with the sweet, nutty taste of Swiss cheese.

FARMHOUSE CHEESE

Surprisingly, cheese was never a mainstay of the Irish diet, even in a country so full of cattle grazing in rich pastures. In the early 1980s, however, the European art of cheesemaking began to be practiced by a handful of farmers who saw it as a way to use up excess milk. The group is now known as CAIS (Irish Farmhouse Cheesemakers Association), and the popularity of Irish farmhouse cheese grows each year. *See also specific cheeses.*

GUBBEEN CHEESE

A washed-rind cheese made by Tom and Giana Ferguson in Schull, County Cork. The Fergusons also make a lightly oak-smoked version in their own smokehouse.

IRISH MIST LIQUEUR

Made from distilled spirits, honey, and herbs, Irish Mist is a popular liqueur for drinking and a flavorful ingredient in cooking.

IRISH WHISKEY MARMALADE

A thick-cut preserve made with oranges and flavored with Irish whiskey.

LOIN OF BACON

see Bacon, loin of.

MEAD

Once the drink of the ancient Gauls and Anglo-Saxons, who made it from fermented honey and water, today, mead is made in Bunratty, County Clare, from white wine, honey, and herbs. Known as Bunratty Meade, it is served as a welcoming drink at the famous medieval castle banquets, but many Irish chefs use it in sauces and desserts.

NETTLES

Bitter, wild greens whose leaves are often cooked in soups and stews.

OATMEAL

One of Ireland's most important cereal crops, oatmeal is used in breads, biscuits, and cakes and also in crusts and toppings. Steel-cut, or pinhead, oats are whole-grain groats (the inner portion of the oat kernel) that have been cut into two or three pieces. Minimal processing helps steel-cut oats to retain their distinctive taste and nutritional value. They're best when you toast them first to bring out their nutty flavor. McCann's Irish Oatmeal is a popular brand.

PINHEAD OATS
see Oatmeal.

POITÍN
Distilled from barley, sugar, and water, poitín was originally made in pot stills over a peat fire. It was banned in Ireland in 1661 and only recently legalized. Bunratty Poitín (also known as potcheen) is now sold throughout the country as well as in the United States. Poitín is sometimes used as a substitute for Irish whiskey.

PORK BELLY
The belly of the pig is the portion that becomes spareribs, bacon, and salt pork. Used to flavor chowders and soups, salt pork is made by covering the belly in salt and letting it cure.

PORTER
see Stout.

RAMPS
Also known as wild onions or wild leeks, ramps can be found from March to June in farmers' markets and in some specialty produce stores.

SMOKED SALMON
Irish salmon is salted, dried, then smoked over an open wood fire or in a kiln either horizontally on trays or suspended over an oak or beechwood fire.

SEA VEGETABLES
Kombu, dulse, hijiki, and other sea vegetables (seaweeds) are popular ingredients in Japanese cookery.

They are sold dried in natural foods stores and Asian markets and usually need to be soaked in cold water for about 10 minutes before use. Ocean Greens is a brand of sea vegetables that contains six varieties.

STEEL-CUT OATS
see Oatmeal.

STOUT
A strong, dark beer made with hops and dark-roasted barley. Guinness and Murphy's are Ireland's most popular stouts. Arthur Guinness renamed stout, originally called porter, for its strong, bold taste.

WHITE PUDDING
White pudding, the most famous of which is made in Clonakilty, County Cork, is a sausage made of ground pork, spices, and oatmeal. It is traditionally served as part of an Irish breakfast.

WHISKEY, IRISH
Irish whiskey undergoes a triple distillation process and a three-year maturation period that distinguishes its flavor from that of Scotch whisky. The oldest whiskey brands are those of the Irish Distillers Group: Jameson, Bushmills, Paddy, and John Powers. The newest brands are Locke's, Tyrconnell, and Kilbeggan, from the reopened Cooley-John Locke's Distillery, Kilbeggan, County Westmeath, and Knappogue Single Malt, named Spirit of the Year in 1999 by *Food & Wine* magazine. Single malts are unblended whiskeys produced in a single distillery from malted barley.

Culahill, County Laois.

ENNISKERRY TRADING CO.

OPEN

OPEN 7 DAYS

TAX FREE

Enniskerry, County Wicklow.

RESOURCES

USE THIS GUIDE to find food and beverages from Ireland or ingredients called for in some recipes.

To find an Irish shop in your area where some of these products are available, contact Enterprise Ireland, 345 Park Avenue, New York, NY, 10154, 212-371-3600; or the Irish Food Board, 3316 North Halstead Street, Unit 4, Chicago, IL, 60657, 773-871-6749.

For details on Irish festivals, contact the Irish Tourist Board, 345 Park Avenue, New York, NY, 10154, 1-800-223-6470.

BUTTER AND CHEESE
To find out which supermarkets sell Irish butter and Kerrygold cheeses, including Dubliner, Kerrygold Swiss, Blarney, and Vintage Cheddar, contact the Irish Dairy Board, 825 Green Bay Road, Suite 200, Wilmette, IL, 60091, 847-256-8289, or visit www.idbusa.com. Kerrygold is the international trademark of the Irish Dairy Board (An Bord Bainne).

To buy Kerrygold cheeses online, contact Traditional Irish Foods, 1-877-IRISHFOOD, or visit www.foodireland.com

To buy Irish farmhouse cheeses online, contact Murrays Cheese Shop, 1-888-692-4339, or visit www.murrayscheese.com; James Cook Cheese Company, 206-256-0510, or visit www.jamescookcheese.com; Andrea London's World of Cheese, 1-800-980-9603, or visit www.worldofcheese.com; or visit www.igourmet.com.

COOKIES, BISCUITS, CRACKERS, TEA, AND COFFEE
To buy cookies, crackers, shortbreads, tea, and coffee online, or to request a catalogue, contact Bewley Irish Imports, 1-800-BEWLEY, or visit www.bewleyirishimports.com; Irish Express, 1-561-219-0664, or visit www.irish-food.com; or Life of Riley Irish Imports, www.loririshimports.com.

CONDIMENTS

To order chutney, honey, jam, jelly, marmalade, preserves, and Irish whole-grain mustards online, or to request a mail-order catalogue, contact Bewley Irish Imports, 1-800-BEWLEY, or visit www.bewleyirishimports.com; or Irish Express, 1-561-219-0664, or visit www.irish-food.com.

FILO DOUGH

Athens Brand Mini Fillo Dough Shells are available in the frozen food section of most supermarkets.

GAME

To order pheasant, rabbit, and venison online, contact D'Artagnan, 1-800-327-8246, or visit www.dartagnan.com; or contact Adirondack Venison Company (loin chops, medallions, racks, roasts, stew meat), 1-800-500-9064, or visit www.avenison.com.

MEAD

To find out where you can buy authentic Irish mead (bottled as Bunratty Meade), contact Camelot Importing Co., 1-800-4-CAMELOT.

MEAT

To order premium-quality lamb (chops, legs, shanks, racks), contact Jamison Farm, 1-800-237-5262, or visit www.jamisonfarm.com.

To order premium-quality beef, lamb, and pork, including pork belly, contact Niman Ranch, 1-510-808-0340, or visit www.nimanranch.com.

To order Irish pork products, including bacon, ham, sausages, and black and white pudding, contact Dairygold U.S.A., 1-800-386-7577, or visit www.dairygold.com; or Traditional Irish Foods, 1-877-IRISHFOOD, or visit www.foodireland.com

OATMEAL

McCann's brand Irish oatmeal is available in most supermarkets. Both McCann's and Odlum's brand are available from Traditional Irish Foods, 1-877-IRISHFOOD, or visit www.foodireland.com; and Oisin Foods, www.oisin.com.

SALMON

To order oak-smoked Irish salmon online, contact Traditional Irish Foods, 1-877-IRISHFOOD, or visit www.foodireland.com. To order directly from smokehouses in Ireland, visit the Burren Smokehouse (organic salmon), www.burrensmokehouse.ie; Kenmare Smoked Salmon, www.kenmaresalmon.com; Kinvara Smoked Salmon (organic salmon), www.kinvara-smoked-salmon.com; Ummera Wild Smoked Salmon, www.ummera.com; or Hederman Smoked Salmon (natural), 01-353-21-481-1089; fax 011-353-21-4814-323.

WILD AND EXOTIC VEGETABLES

To order ramps or fresh wild mushrooms online, contact Marché aux Delices, 1-888-547-5471, or visit www.auxdelices.com; to order dried wild mushrooms, visit www.jrmushroomsandspecialties.com.

Gallagher's Restaurant,
Bunratty, County Clare.

INDEX

TABLE OF EQUIVALENTS

THE EXACT EQUIVALENTS in the following tables
have been rounded for convenience.

LIQUID/DRY MEASURES

U.S.	Metric
¼ teaspoon	1.25 milliliters
½ teaspoon	2.5 milliliters
1 teaspoon	5 milliliters
1 tablespoon (3 tsp)	15 milliliters
1 fluid ounce (2 tbsp)	30 milliliters
¼ cup	60 milliliters
⅓ cup	80 milliliters
½ cup	120 milliliters
1 cup	240 milliliters
1 pint (2 cups)	480 milliliters
1 quart (4 cups, 32 ounces)	960 milliliters
1 gallon (4 quarts)	3.84 liters
1 ounce (by weight)	28 grams
1 pound	454 grams
2.2 pounds	1 kilogram

OVEN TEMPERATURE

Fahrenheit	Celsius	Gas
250°	120°	½
275°	140°	1
300°	150°	2
325°	160°	3
350°	180°	4
375°	190°	5
400°	200°	6
425°	220°	7
450°	230°	8
475°	240°	9
500°	260°	10

LENGTH

U.S.	Metric
⅛ inch	3 millimeters
¼ inch	6 millimeters
½ inch	12 millimeters
1 inch	2.5 centimeters